Filipino Satire

A COMPENDIUM OF RESEARCH-BASED ARTICLES ON CULTURAL IDIOCIES AND INTELLECTUAL HUMOR

Sherill Asis-Gilbas

Filipino Satire

A Compendium of Research-based Articles on
Cultural Idiocies and Intellectual Humor

Copyright @2021 by

Sherill Asis-Gilbas

ISBN 978-1-257-90719-9

Published by Lulu Book Publishing

United States of America

Dedication

To Daddy Rey, Shaine, RL, Shine and Reinne,

May you continue to enjoy life and laugh intellectually.

To laugh is to think of others' needs, too.

SAG

Acknowledgments

The author is forever grateful to the support of the Sorsogon State University, Commission on Higher Education, her family, friends, and relatives.

To God be the Glory.

CONTENTS

Preface

This book is another compilation of five research articles. The literary materials used are novels of a transnational writer, *Merlinda Bobis*. Each article employed different approaches, but all focused on identifying the satirical aspects that unravel Filipino culture, beliefs, practices, and traditions.

The first article intended to present the Filipino Satire used as an aesthetic expression of needs relative to socio-cultural and political issues and concerns from the Early Philippine Novel in English to the contemporary works of expatriate writers. Defamiliarization and Humor theories, including Social Criticism, are used as the main frameworks of this paper, which are descriptive, analytical, and qualitative.

The second article employed Freud and Lacan's Psychoanalyzes particularly on the pleasure and reality principles. Likewise, the cultural and gender studies and semiotics were applied in the treatment of material. This descriptive-qualitative type of analysis employed on the novel highlights how cultural-domestic issues and socio-political problems brought along by poverty.

Furthermore, the material used in the third article is *Banana Heart Summer*. The article sought to describe the novel's theme, tone, structure, and style, as well as the socio-political and cultural aspects using food as primary trope. It also aimed to present the reality frame of the depicted societal problems of the Filipinos in general and those of Bicolanos in particular. The formalist theory was applied in the treatment of material, which is a satire. The defamiliarization theory was employed through devices such as tropes and social realism.

The fourth article used formalistic approach in the literary analysis of the elements of fiction, contextual representation of star as the novel's trope, and the societal problems depicted in the novel. It aimed to introduce a paper that may be used in a teaching-learning scenario that evaluates and criticizes, anchored on the philosophical theory of Lacan on psychoanalysis. Finally, the last article asserts that a piece of literature reflects the worldview of its writer, which is the result of personal experiences, basically rooted from culture. Bobis sees her country's need for liberation and search for cultural strength. Her being transnational motivates her to write from her perspective of Philippine culture associated with her personal experiences in another country. She wants her readers to understand the novels from the recognition of society behind the creative representation of political and cultural flaws.

To reiterate, this book hoped to impart real-life ideas from the product of fiction, to treat creative works not only as a reading material for pleasure but with intellectual gusto. All the articles in this book aims to promote the tools of satire to be considered as effective methods of explaining and understanding Filipino culture. May Filipinos retain their love for reading, understand their cultural and communal humor and do necessary action towards the general welfare.

1

Filipino Satire: Expression of Needs from Early Philippine Novels to Contemporary Works

Published in American Journal of Humanities and Social Science Research
e-ISSN 2378-703X Volume 5 Issue 7

ABSTRACT

A Filipino literary icon asserts that satire is a form of Literature. This paper intends to present the Filipino Satire used as an aesthetic expression of needs relative to socio-cultural and political issues and concerns from the Early Philippine Novel in English to the contemporary works of expatriate writers. Defamiliarization and Humor theories, including Social Criticism, are used as the main frameworks of this paper, which are descriptive, analytical and qualitative. In this paper, Filipino satire is grouped into five: (1) domestic/marital satire, (2) cultural satire, (3) satire on religion, (4) political satire, and (5) satire on Filipinism. The aesthetic expression lies in the tone and form. This paper concluded that Filipino satire appeals to the intellect and culture based despite its being underrated. It reveals societal issues in a lighter manner that conceals the darker side of the issue. It differs from comedy because it uses ridicule as a corrective measure while comedy mainly evokes laughter to amuse or entertain. It is recommended to consider the signification of language, which reveals historical and cultural background in literary works and in conveying lived experiences of an individual, or the community in general.

Keywords: Filipino satire, defamiliarization, humor theory, social criticism

INTRODUCTION

Satire is a form of literature. Its primary role is to ridicule or criticize any subject, idea, institution or mankind in general. The satirist's objective is to expose some representative vices that are considered threatening or harmful to the society. It also aims to point out human behaviour that is despicable and needs to be changed. Its goal can be either destruction or reform but mainly for the general benefit or betterment of humanity.

Abrams (1999) further discusses satire as an incidental element within many works where overall mode is not satiric—in a certain character or situation, or in an interpolated passage of ironic commentary on some aspect of the human condition or of contemporary society. The aesthetics of satire comes through the theme and tone of the literary pieces that carry its object of ridicule.

Accordingly, biographical and psychoanalytic critics inspired by Freud tend to look at satire through the author's perspective, reading it as a product of the author's fears, hates or grudges, or as a manifestation of personality disorder. Others view satire as persuasive rhetoric, with a moral goal to correct folly and to lash vice. Satirists justify its practice as a corrective of human vice and folly. The claim is to ridicule the failing rather than the individual, and to limit its ridicule to corrigible faults, excluding those for which a person is not responsible.

The theories on humor can be associated with the idea of satire. Mulder (2002), in his article disclosed the conventional humor theories. Such theories are superiority theory, relief theory, and incongruity theory. Meanwhile, sociology theories provide insight on the social and cultural context of a joke or any other humorous event. They focus on the way the joke iscontextually interpreted. It means the understanding of a joke is part of many different social actions. **Satire and Comedy**

Satire differs from comedy because the former ridicules and is used as a corrective measure while the latter mainly invokes laughter as to amuse or entertain. People laugh at different things, thus, there is so-called high comedy which evokes "intellectual laughter," or the thoughtful laughter from spectators who remain emotionally detached from the action at the spectacle of folly, pretentiousness, and incongruity in human behavior. This is similar to satire. Low comedy, on the other hand, has no intellectual appeal. It arouses laughter by jokes,and by slapstick humor and boisterous or clownish physical activity. The laughter that appeals to the intellect is the characteristic of satire; while the comic provides humor that can easily beperceived by the senses. The Filipino type of satire is a creative presentation of the societal angst since time immemorial through the literary material, specifically, a novel. The use of satire reflects the biting realities of life yet is revealed in a humorous manner.

Socio-cultural and Political Issues

Social forces refer to the factors that may influence the behavior of an individual or groups in the society. These may include culture and politics. The former is a composition of knowledge, belief, art, morals, law, customs and any other capabilities or habits acquired by the member; while the latter may reflect authority or power of an individual or group inherentfrom the societal aspects. Colon (2010) explains culture as associated with the sociological point of view. It is "an organization of phenomena that are dependent upon symbols; phenomena which include acts (pattern of behaviour), objects (tools and things), ideas (beliefs, knowledge), and sentiments (attitudes, values)" (p.4).

Societal problems are always associated with culture and are political in nature.Literary articles, particularly prose narratives, contain stories that discuss socio-cultural and political issues. This paper considers that narratives provide societal conglomeration of experiences in various ways and styles. The researcher posits that Filipino satire is an artistic expression of the lived experiences of people in a literary or fictive form.

The Material

The novel, which rose with the influence of Western culture, was brought by colonization. Mojares (1983) defines novel as a fictional prose narrative of a certain extent. He emphasizes that the word *narrative* requires the presence of a story and a storyteller. EarlyFilipino novels have clear manifestations of said influences such as those of Paterno's and Rizal's. The works of these two Filipino novelists in Spanish generally served as outstanding legacy of the novel in the Philippines from which the modern novel of today can trace its themeand form. Hence, novels serve as a good material of the satirists. Thus justified, this paper utilizes the novel as the main tool of Filipino satire as aesthetic manifestation of socio-culturaland political concerns.

According to Lumbera, (1997) reading a literary work requires one to engage with its language as the social practice of individuals, groups and institutions. He refers to Philippine literature as that which "may be produced in the capital city of Manila and in the different urbancenters and rural outposts, even in foreign lands where descendants of Filipino migrants use English or any of the languages of the Philippines to create works that tell about their lives andaspirations" (p2). This goes to show that the novels though written in another country and in aforeign language may still serve as good sources of material on Philippine studies. Furthermore, Lumbera says:

> *The forms used by Filipino authors may be indigenous or borrowed from other cultures, and these may range from popular pieces addressed to mass audiences to highly sophisticated works intended for the intellectual elite.* (p. 2)

Galdon(1985), enumerates women writers who have played

significant roles in the development of Philippine writing in English. In his essay which was also published in the book that he edited, *Essays on The Philippine Novel in English*, he identifies nostalgia as one of the more frequent themes of contemporary Philippine writers in English. In addition, he has observed that Philippine writing often highlights the idyllic nostalgia or longing for home in the provinces, which he considers either gentle or bitterly satiric. Specifically, Lumbera (1997)defines nostalgia this way:

> *Nostalgia is the melancholy longing for home, or the wistful and often sentimental yearning for a real or romanticized past that cannot be regained. It is often characterized by innocence, even by naivete in ironic conjunction with manipulative cleverness, authentic simplicity and a quality of frustrated aspiration which characterizes dreamland* (pp. 96- 97)

Indeed, novels are intended to arouse emotions by allowing readers to make intellectual discoveries of ideals creatively embedded in the writer's artistry through thematic presentation, form, style, and general structure of the work. These discoveries also lead them to decipher ideas, which can enlighten, inspire, or simply inform them accordingly.

THEORETICAL BACKGROUND

This paper anchors on the defamiliarization and humor theories and the use of social criticism. As Abrams (1999) explains, when applied in literature, defamiliarization works in three levels—on the level of language, on the level of content, and on the level of literary forms.The novels under study therefore have the application of the three levels.

One of the techniques in defamiliarization is magic realism. It is when the author uses realism in representing ordinary events and descriptive details together with fantastic and dreamlike elements, as well as with materials derived from myths and fairy tales.

Another technique is the use of social realism, which refers to novels reflecting social reality stressing the oppression of workers by bourgeois capitalist, where the virtues of the proletariat and the struggle between economic classes are the essential dynamics of the society.

Meyer (2000) asserts that humor is used to unify as well as to divide. He cites *tease* asan example where it is viewed as humorous and aggressive at the same time. The recipient's prior relationship with the teaser will decide whether the message is "primarily a tension- relieving mood lightener or a lightly disguised critique" (p310)

Social critics, as explained by Makaryk (1993), is a term used to distinguish literature that addresses specific political, social, economic, cultural, or religious issues. The writers whose works contain social criticism hope to do more than merely entertain readers. Social critics are individuals who present by-products of a larger activity, the cultural elaboration and affirmation of their collective reflection of the community or society they represent as a collective life. Their reasons for addressing political and social problems may vary, but most of them feel a responsibility to make readers aware of certain facts.

Background of the Filipino Novel

Mojares (1983) studies the Filipino novel with historical approach and arrives at a "diachronic as well as a synchronic estimation" (p2) of the Filipino novel. He concluded that a novel acquires its own kind from its specific society. Culture and history are important contributory factors where the narrative evolves. He summarily describes the background of Filipino novel in the following statements:

There is a complex background to the Filipino novel. While it reflects its indebtedness to the Western novel, it also has its roots in native soil, in a local tradition of narratives: on one hand, epics, ballads, tales and other folk narratives; on the other hand, the inchoate mass of narratives or 'proto-novels'-

metrical romances, lives of saints, moral and social tracts, and others which, while inspired by foreign models, had in the course of time been naturalized on the home grounds. (p.367)

The Early Novels in the Philippines (Spanish regime)

According to Hornedo (2004), the first concept of novel in the Philippines came through the *Urbana at Felisa* of P. Modesto de Castro in 1864. It was followed by *Ninay* in 1885 by Pedro A. Paterno. This novel is intended to expose ignorance, superstition, and oppression in the Philippines. Two years later, the first novel of Jose Rizal, *Noli Me Tangere*, was published in 1887, followed by its sequel, *El Filibusterismo* in 1891. Critics have noted the similarity of the *Noli* to the work of Benito Perez Galdos' *Doña Perfecta*, which Hornedo describes as "a strong social satire."

In the book *Ideas and Ideals*, Hornedo clarifies that the Filipino novel in Spanish appears only after the first novelists had left their native Philippines and had stayed for a while in Spain. In the same book, Hornedo enumerates the elements of the Spanish literary tradition that have influenced the birth of the Filipino novel in Spanish. They are: *The costumbrismo in Spanish narrative; Social criticism; The novel as genre; and Krausismo.*

Costumbrismo refers to both genre and movement. It is an important aspect of romanticism that must be clearly distinguished from earlier depiction of customs and manners. Accordingly, the general features of costumbrismo are difficult to characterize because of their wide variety of both Spanish and European forms. It can be traced back to Spain's history. During the 19th Century, the Imperial Spain was sharply divided between conservatives and liberals, as well as rural and urban society. The Provincial Spain, where the Philippines was one of the provinces, totally lost its support from the Imperial Spain in 1815. Thus, the Spaniards became acquisitive and greedy. According to Mojares, Rizal's novels contain references to the comedia and moro-moro, Baltazar, and such works as *Urbana and Feliza* and*Tandang Basio Macunat.*

In the Philippine literary perspective, the idea of costumbrismo refers to literary or pictorial interpretation of local everyday life, mannerisms, and customs, primarily in the Hispanic scene in the 19th Century. It is related to artistic realism and Romanticism, often satiric and even moralizing. At times, its approach deals on quaint folkloric tale and often hasa romanticizing aspect.

Hornedo describes costumbrismo as short sketches of types and customs. They were vignettes and short pictorial descriptions. Plots were often mere excuses for the description ofthe country customs; and even when the plot was the main interest, it was often interrupted by the description of peculiar customs rendered in objective detail". The traces of the early literaryforms in the novels of the Filipino writers in Spanish showcase the idea of custombrismo.

Objectives

This study aimed to identify and analyze the use of Filipino satire as an aesthetics expression of needs related to socio-cultural and political issues and concerns. Specifically, itprobes on the basic influential factors to the Philippine novel from the Spanish to American and to the contemporary period, giving focus on the three contemporary novels of Merlinda Bobis. It intended to cite the presence of satire in the works of Filipino writers as their artistic way of presenting the society's political and cultural concerns. This paper also posited that Filipino satire is different from the other known types of satire, such as Horatian and Juvenalian.

METHODOLOGY

This paper uses a descriptive-qualitative presentation of ideas. It also makes use of literary criticism and analytical approach to decipher the use of defamiliarization and humor theories as well as social criticism.

The researcher traces the use of satire in the Filipino novels from the early Philippine novel in Spanish and in English to the contemporary works of the expatriate writers. The selection of novels does not basically deal on the author but on the materials that were publishedduring the Spanish Regime and those early novels written by Filipinos. Representative materials during the American period were provided to identify the presence and use of satire in every work. They were chosen as representative of the period in terms of its societal recognition. The background of the Filipino novel is also discussed for a holistic comprehension.

The works of expatriate writers after the American regime were also analyzed to showthat satire is still of use in contemporary works. The three novels of Bobis[i]—*Banana Heart Summer, The Solemn Lantern Maker,* and the *Fish Hair Woman*—were used to identify the useof Filipino satire as aesthetic expression on societal, cultural, and political issues. The theme and tone expect to reveal in the general form of the three novels a critique of the society with the use of tropes and signification.

The traditional satirical techniques are exaggeration, incongruity, parody, reversal, and defamiliarization. From the analyses of the said novels, the particular types of Filipino satire were named based on the identified characteristics as a result of this paper.

RESULTS AND DISCUSSION

Satire in the Filipino Novels in Spanish

Rizal's two novels are satirical, employing two different but complementary satirical approaches. The first refers to the writing of characters or types of people to whom one ascribesin exaggerated caricature humorous and ridiculous patterns of behavior. The second form is not focused on the characters but in the depiction of typical scenes or situations that serve as representation of unhealthy status of existing social relations. *Don Tiburcio*, the quack doctor, and the nostalgic relations of the students and their life in Manila are examples of how Rizal employed satire. His use of satire in the novels was considered a non-violent protest against the current state of affairs in his home country.

The novels of Rizal, as one of the pioneers in this field as a Filipino novelist in Spanish,show his native background and the influence of European literary tradition. In his novels, Rizal uses the treatment of issue as element to introduce social criticism. While Paterno's *Ninay* features the then-contemporary Filipino society, romantically exhibiting players inside and outside the politico-religious authority structure of the colonial order, Rizal, on the other hand,criticizes Philippine culture through political analysis. *Noli* brought to bear the fact that Spainhad failed to recreate a humanist society out of its colony.

Furthermore, Hornedo posits that the two novels of Rizal are *jeremiads*. They are intended "to warn the Spain to right the wrongs and save the Philippines from the freebooters who were trying to rob her of her colony and of the Filipinos their dignity and liberties."[ii] Theyreflect the fears and interests of the *ilustrado* class who, accordingly, has little understanding of the "real and potential for action" of the non-*ilustrado* class. It was clarified that the novels' theme highlights the "Philippine inefficient government dominated and manipulated by greedy friars" that creates "ineffectual and unproductive citizenry," thus, may be unhealthy to the part of Spain. The criticism does not actually favor the Philippines, but the novels were treated theother way around.

Satire in the Early Philippine Novels in English

Zoilo M. Galang was the first Filipino novelist in English. His *A Child of Sorrow* published in 1921 is the first Philippine novel written in English. He wrote both in English andthe vernacular. Galdon (1969) identifies three romantic themes in the fiction of Galang, such as, imagination and mystery, the happy throb of the tender passions, and didacticism. His othernovel called *A Novel of Filipino Life* with the original title, *Visions of the Sower*, published in 1924, has the main theme of labor, success, and patriotism.

It can be deemed that *A Child of Sorrow* is pioneer in the field of novels in English in the Philippines. Continuing this literary tradition with the English language, Galang used scriptural aphorisms, name symbols, and social moralizing. There are also flashes of social criticism that can be somehow regarded as satire.

One of the novels that followed Galang's is Maximo Kalaw's, *The Filipino Rebel,* published in 1930. Doreen Fernandez claims that Kalaw has the same consciousness of Rizal in his *Noli* and *Fili* although the former lacks the texture, details, and scope of the latter's novels. To quote Mojares, "the *Filipino Rebel* is in the tradition of Rizal, but lacking in the force and finesse in terms of imagination, falters in the formal integration of factual and historical material."[iii] Thus, considering the novel's limited literary lineage, the novel may havesome hints of satirical device focusing on the political, social milieu.

Another novelist is Juan C. Laya. His first novel made him an instant celebrity when *His Native Soil* won for him first prize in the First Commonwealth Literary Contest in 1940. Emmanuel Torres describes the tone of Laya's novel that somehow works in a disarmingly naïve way to serve the cultural setting, the rural/folk culture of his Ilocano characters,descendants of several generations of farmers in Pangasinan. He made effort at writing the novel with many, big subjects (customs, history, current events, cultural ideas) going on at once. Torres concluded that by writing Laya's two novels, he kept alive the tradition of sociallyconscious literature, of which Rizal's *Noli* and *Fili* are the classic prototypes.

Indications of satire are present in his characters such as the corrupt, philandering Abogado Murcia and the flirtatious but harmless American-mestiza Virgina Fe. It is also evident in Martin, the main character who returns to Pangasinan after acquiring formal education in the United States. He has difficulty speaking in his native language, Ilocano, and disappoints everyone when he switches to English during the reception for high school graduates.

In addition, Mojares (1983) opines that *His Native Soil* echoes the interest in social problems of the 1930s and is expressive of two themes that preoccupied writers of Laya's generation. These two themes are: the tensions of a society in the throes of modernization, andthe need for a viable accommodation of Western values and native mores.

Stevan Javellana's *Without Seeing the Dawn* published in 1947 can be likened to Paterno's *Ninay*. Soledad Reyes[iv] notes that while Paterno had the Spaniards of the nineteenthcentury, Javellana had the Americans of the twentieth century. It is a story of local color, of customs and scenes meant to show that Filipinos have a culture of their own. The novel tries to shed light on unionism more than any other institution in the city. It reveals some sordid aspects of city life, unrelieved poverty, loss of traditional values, the prevalence of vice, and an overwhelming sense of decay and death. His protagonist Carding is depicted as naturally resilient, endowed with almost boundless optimism, despite a series of frustrating setbacks suchas betrayal, death, destruction, loss of land—a pathetic victim of life. His name, Ricardo Suerteis ironic of what life offers him, which is an implication of a satirical technique.

F. Sionil Jose's *The Pretenders* in 1962 belongs to the post-war novels, which portray the image of the Filipino as a wanderer. It has an abundance of stories and novels depicting thelives of expatriates and their terrible sense of isolation in foreign lands. The novel is set in thecity and talks about the memory of an idyllic barrio life, which sustains the main character Tony Samson, a historian who wants to retrieve the lost past that the barrio represents. The satirical flavor in the novel is the reversal of the traditional growth from innocence to experience, or from the barrio to the city. It is an account of how the protagonist attempts to redeem himself by returning to his roots.

A Season of Grace, released in 1963 by N.V.M. Gonzales, also suggests a streakof satire through the use of malevolent symbols that can be taken as a defamiliarizing technique—the fresh fish, screeching owl, the shell, the hawk, the rats, and the tall *dao* tree. The year of grace in the novel showed the absence of fresh fish except when the rats came. Quite similar to the Filipino rebel, the theme of this novel seems to be the all-enduring man and nature.

But for the Lovers by Wilfrido Nolledo, a novel published in 1970 in New York, usesa conglomeration of language such as English, Tagalog, *Chabakano*, Ilustrado Spanish, Japanese, and *kanto boy lingo*. It is the first in a projected trilogy of novels about the Philippines. The novel is described by Georgina Reyes as having a "phantasmagoric quality resulting from the counterpointing and juxtaposition of reality and illusion, actual incident anddream, memories and hallucinations." The satirical hint in the novel is reflected in the Filipinolife during the occupation years, which include haunting images of wraithlike figures desperately roaming the streets in search of food, images of Luneta and Intramuros, accounts of torture in Fort Santiago, enactments of rituals, catalogs of Filipino delicacies, and *haranas*.

Satire in the Contemporary Novels of Merlinda Bobis[v]

Tone: Tone indicates the mood or attitude of the persona in the narrative. It helps identify themessage or the purpose of the author in writing the story. The general tone of the three novelsis satiric. They all present societal problems that need attention and solution. They all call for immediate help. Though blatantly satirical, the tone can be categorized into degrees, with the first novel having subtle satire, the second novel, moderate and the third, bitter satire.

All the three novels have satirical tone loaded with Filipino customs and practices. The Filipinoculture is used as the object of satire where the beliefs on superstitions, traditions, religious practices, myths and legends are the focal point. The socio-political aspect is also exposed through the representation of the characters as officers in the government. Bobis uses cultural and socio-political aspects as vehicles to ridicule practices that people in other places and even in the Philippines may either find helpful or destructive.

Though satirical in tone and presented in a nostalgic way in general, every novel suggests a different mood. *Banana Heart Summer* presents a domestic and rural ambiance through the narration of a child. It is full of optimism and hope and focuses on simple pleasures. The secondnovel, *The Solemn Lantern Maker* is urban centered with some flashes of a farm life that provide obvious contrast and similarity between the two. The desperate hope of those in the city fearing eviction from their "borrowed lands" and their way of life presents a resemblance with that of those in the rural, in the farm, cultivating one's land for their living. The novel calls for hope despite the traumatic experiences from the societal cancer, the hegemony of power. The third novel, *Fish-Hair Woman* offers a darker and grim mood. The three decades and transcontinental scope are filled with the idea of searching. The search for identity, love, acceptance, and justice is presented through the ideas of insanity, torture, and death.

The satiric tone in the novels of Bobis serves as a corrective of societal folly. Readers are taskedto decode the hidden message in the nostalgic discussion of the writer by exposing the socio- cultural and political journey of her mother country, the Philippines. As Hornedo (2001) puts it in the concluding part of his essay, *Political Jokes: Evasion and Resistance*: "A large numberof Filipinos are not happy about how things are being run in this country. The jokes, of course, suggest no alternative program of action. But they can certainly and plainly identify the personswho must own some moral responsibility for whatever is that Filipinos these past years do not like in their national life" (p229). It simply reflects what Bobis, in a way, would like to tell Filipinos and other nationalities.

Theme: Theme, on the other hand, is defined by Abrams as "usefully applied to a general concept or doctrine, whether implicit or asserted, which an imaginative work is designed to incorporate and make persuasive to the reader" (Abrams,p.170).

The three novels' thematic aspect deals mostly with the issues that arise from socio-cultural and political problems. They are presented in the table below:

Table 1. The themes of the novel

Novels	Themes
Banana Heart Summer	Poverty—material, spiritual, emotional; An appeal for awareness and human interaction
The Solemn Lantern Maker	Freedom—rights to speak, to be heard, to choose, to have peace, to live comfortably
Fish-Hair Woman	Oppression— incidental and intentional; A revolutionary call for justice

From the individual theme of each novel, it can be synthesized that the universal theme of love still prevails. The theme of poverty in the first novel can be traced back to the pursuit of love. The material, spiritual, and emotional poverty may be eased through the fulfilment of each of the characters' various desires. Parental love is what the protagonist longed to feel while the other characters search for the love that accepts their individual needs and respects their differences.

The theme of freedom and identity in the second novel can also be hinted from the idea of love. This is clearly evident in the major character's trauma. It resulted in Nolan's *silence* which can be traced back to his father's love. The arrival of the American, Cate Burns, who was called the *angel*, was triggered by her love for her unborn child. The love for *peace* of the other characters manipulated their actions and connivance to the extent of sabotage and salvage.

In the third novel, love is also the probable cause of every event and action of the characters. The narrator's love for her village obliges her to claim herself as the *fish-hair woman*. Her intention is to liberalize the victims of oppression and provide justice through stories written from her memory.

The narratives of Bobis are communicators of Philippine culture and history that emanate from the type of love that the Filipino has to offer and has yet to have. She uses the characters and events, although fictive in revealing the ugly points of Filipinos. According to Hornedo (2000) in his overview of Anthropology, "every cultural community, large or small,understands itself in the frame of its own narrative or account of itself. All cultures are assumed to have their own narratives of themselves. To understand them is to understand their narrative(Hornedo, pp.70-71).

Moreover, based from his discussion of the theory and the genesis of literary text, it was explained that the creation of a literary work is guided consciously or unconsciously by what the author thinks literature ought to achieve, to be made of, to look like and by whom. Hence, Bobis' novels appeal to the reading Filipinos to act on their societal problems presentedin a literary way through intellectual humor, not only to laugh at their own idiocies. Likewise,she also targets other reading nationalities for possible support.

The Philippine Societal Problems in the Novels

The three novels of Bobis are filled with numerous and various societal problems that are literarily and creatively presented. The analysis of each novel reveals common problems that resulted from political and cultural factors such as poverty, immorality, child labor, corruption, and hegemony of power.

Below is the table that presents the societal problems deciphered from each novel.

Table 2. Socio cultural and political concerns in the novel

Novels	Socio-cultural and Political Issues
Banana Heart Summer	Child abuse/Child Labor, Poverty, Employment Problem, Corruption, Immorality
The Solemn Lantern Maker	Poverty, Gambling, Corruption, Child Prostitution, OFW Blues, Immorality, Hegemony of Power
Fish-Hair Woman	Abuse of Power, Poverty, Immorality, Corruption, Insurgency

Such hegemony or abuse of power and the corruption of the

elected politicians cause poverty, which results in child labor, child prostitution, immorality, gambling, and OFW issues. Likewise, the rebellion or insurgency problem is an offshoot of the government-relatedconcern.

Philippine culture, in general, affects the totality of the societal problems. It is on that thought where Bobis might have anchored her novels. She utilized culture as the object of satireto literarily and creatively unveil the problems that resulted from socio-political agenda. She invokes intellectual laughter to the readers who may or may not be aware of Philippine culture.For instance, the religiosity of the Filipinos against their poverty problem is presented in an incongruous way through the posted reminder in the church which says, "To all dear parishioners, please do not leave your personal belongings unattended; somebody might thinkthey're the 'answer' to their prayers." The said reminder indirectly reveals that there are Filipino thieves even in a sacred place.

Another obvious example of how Bobis presents a serious socio-political problem is through symbolic presentation of the characters. The hope of the fatherland, the children are her major characters in the three novels who all desire to help their family. The youth represents hope and cure to the ills of the society. Despite their innocence and young age, they all offer the best service they can to augment their family's poverty. Nining and Noland tried to help bring food to their families' tables while Estrella and Luke helped to give justice to their families. Nining became an OFW and gave up schooling while Noland was traumatized and became a victim of a pedophile while Estrella lost her life after killing her own father.

In the article of Hornedo on the conceptual structure of the relationship of theory to literary text, he posits that "the literary text is not a creation in a vacuum, but a contexted creature rooted in a society through the author and shaped by the writer's philosophy or theory of what literature ought to be and to do." [vi] On this premise, the creative works of Bobis intendto reveal the societal problems through invoking laughter that suggests awareness and concernof her readers.

The Techniques and Devices of Satire in the Novels

The three novels are packed with satirical techniques and devices. These devices and techniques include exaggeration, incongruity, parody, reversal, and defamiliarization.

Exaggeration technique is employed by Bobis in the three novels through the description of characters, incident, and overstatement about certain ideas. In the first novel, the exaggeration'sfocus is on the characters of Tiya Asun and Senora Ching and the idea that hunger results in the lengthening of the esophagus. In the second novel, it is the "creation of land" at the wave of a hand of the First Lady, and the ordinary notebook of a ten-year old mute was claimed as an evidence of a conspiracy of a terrorist attack. The third novel's use of exaggeration is shownin the description of the hair, its length and use. It was said to be twelve meters long and is usedto trawl corpses from the river.

The use of incongruity is also observable in the three novels. In the *Banana Heart Summer*, the ironic circumstances are depicted during the time of volcanic eruption and the death by suicide of one of the characters. The time of crisis is still considered as an opportunity to improve the economic situation of the village as foreign aid will abound in the community,making the politician acquire another mansion. The person's death by suicide because of desperation triggers generosity among those who previously withheld their help. In *The Solemn Lantern Maker*, one example of incongruity is presented in the mention of a televisionshow with twenty-five thousand people vying for instant prizes such as cash, car, or even a house. The promise of joy and hope turns out as a tragic incident as many people either died and got hurt during the stampede. In the *Fish-Hair Woman*, incongruity is exhibited when a political figure uses the phrase, "my house" to claim a place that he just "borrowed." Incongruous, too, is the labeling of a dumb person as "the terrible."

Parody is also common in the three novels as a defamiliarizing strategy because of its focus on peculiarities. Bobis works on the dilly song or game of children. She substitutes or changes the lyrics to another. The names of biblical characters are also used as reference to another, which suggests travesty, a type of parody.

The use of reversal is also a technique applied in the novel. The tropes used in the threenovels are the opposite of the suggested theme of each novel. The idea of a child who supportsthe family, instead of the parents is another example.

Bobis' creative use of defamiliarization opens the reader to the possibility of understanding the culture of the community represented by the novel's setting. The aestheticsof satire intends to create realization from the reader's point of view to appreciate the work offiction, and at the same time to be mindful of the biting realities of life. All the three novels are full of lines that reveal thoughtful concerns presented in a way that the reader shall find amusingyet needs to be changed. The Bicolanos[vii] are Filipinos whose ideas and ideals may emanate from their inherent desires and their promulgation rooted from the type of culture that they have. Just as Rizal's novels satirize the Filipino's characters and attitudes against Spaniards, Bobis' novel also aims to call for a change and positivity amidst the cultural idiocies of the Filipinos, particularly Bicolanos.

Filipino Satire

Based from the identified satirical techniques and devices in the novels, the researcherregrouped and identified the satirical devices and techniques that can be called Filipino satire.Bobis' novels are filled with examples of ridiculous ideas and instances that suggest distinct Filipinos' initial source of humor. Said instances after the initial laugh will invoke thinking fora possible remedy to the object, person, or idea being ridiculed. Such problems are rooted in culture and inherent to their local ways of life.

These are the identified types of Filipino satire:

Domestic/Marital Satire:

This type of satire refers to the ideas that reflect humor about married life and the Filipino family's orientation. From the first novel, Maring, Nining's mother is called "rice cooked too soon."[viii] This is because she eloped with a mason when she was just a 14-year-old, first year high school. This resulted in having six babies "that come out of the armpit."[ix] Another consequence is the "silence" of her husband, Gable which Nining regarded as "tongue eaten by the devil."[x]

From the Filipino family's orientation, the proper marrying age is 20 years old and above, after finishing formal education. It is also a practice that the father supports the family's finances and mainly decides on the family issues. Whenever those expectations are not met, either way, gender roles based on the society's expectations become the object of ridicule and out-of-proportion criticism.

Cultural Satire

This type refers to the customs and beliefs, traditions, and habitual practices of Filipinos that may be considered ridiculous. The ideas on myths, legends, and supernatural and superstitious beliefs that are evident in the narratives are the object of this type of satire. For instance, the itch, which was apparently caused by the spirit in the river called *Onglo*, was the reason for the death of Carmen, the protagonist's mother in the third novel. It was in the river where she met Mayor Kiko, who got her pregnant at the age of fourteen. The coincidental facts are being related to the beliefs of rural people on supernatural spirits to give explanation and point fingers at for someone's misfortune.

Satire on Religion

Some Catholic practices are also subject of satire. They are considered "religious" because they are church/bible based. For instance, the reminder in the church which read, "Be careful of your belongings, someone may think they are the answers to their prayers," is a clearmanifestation that even churchgoers cannot be fully trusted. The place of worship, such as theQuiapo Church, becomes a center of commerce where everything can be bought, including items that kill unborn children. Those Catholic practices are being criticized in a light and literary manner in this type of satire.

Political Satire

Just like political jokes, this type of Filipino satire functions as a tool to communicate and express people's sentiments through the ridicule of powerful people, making them subjectof humor.

One of the common societal problems in the three narratives is the issue of corruption.The politician characters are used as subject of ridicule, such as the town mayor in the first novel, Senator GB in the second novel, and the mayor-turned-congressman Kiko in the third novel. These three characters all faced life's turmoil and defeat and eventually had theirrespective fall out of power.

Satire on Filipinism

This type refers to the English and Filipino words that are either re- defined or assigned different meaning, double meanings, or change of pronunciation. This is the Filipino version of pun.

One of the characters in the *Fish-Hair Woman* is called 'holarawnd', referring to beinga jack of all trades. It was based from the phrase, "all around." From the narrative, Pay Inyo has various occupations in the village such as, a 'herbularyo,' a gravedigger, a small-time businessman, and even the 'secret keeper'. Thus, he earned the title of 'holarawnd'. The criticism is provided in the in-depth meaning of the character's name. The same thing is true to the 'sweet potato king', or 'Bolodoy da teribol' a translation of the English title, "the terrible". His real name, Rizalino, was patterned from the country's national hero, Jose Rizal. His character manifests a dumb person whose hopes and life were wasted despite his being skilled in raising the sweetest potatoes and catching giant eels. Those character labels illustratethis type of satire.

Works of other Expatriate Writers

Carlos Bulosan and Bienvenido Santos are some of the early expatriate writers in America whose writings are filled with satirical techniques. Their works depict the lives of Filipinos abroad and mirror the rural-urban dichotomy. Their works of fiction, such as *Americais in the Heart* and *You Lovely People*, have evidential analysis of sociological values and slice of Filipino life. Accordingly, Bulosan exposed the weaknesses of the Filipinos and pointed out their habitual influence, the insatiable thirst for gambling, their blind acceptance of and admiration for foreign things, and the graft of those in power aside from the greed of the rich. Another expatriate writer is Alejandro Roces, who is called a 'writer by accident' because he wrote thinking only that his stories could be possible materials of his fiction writer friend. Meanwhile, Roseburg examined seven of his stories and found that all of them are humorous. Sy confirms that "Alejandro Roces' short fiction inherently reveals humor in its formalistic elements that satirize peculiar Filipinism."[xi] This is an example of how she discussed that humor was revealed in Roces' work through conflict:

In "We Filipinos are Mild Drinkers," the conflict unfolds the drinking contest betweenthe proud American and the unassuming Filipino. Humor, with the utilization of mild satire, irony, simile and allusion, is presented in the form of unexpected effects like the American during the first and second gulp of the native wine thinks that he "has swallowed a centipede"and that "his tie is his tongue." Because of heavy intoxication, he then falsely accuses the Filipino as the bomber of Pearl Harbor. This humorous depiction of the American is at the sametime ridiculing his unwholesome attitude of feeling superior to Filipinos in terms of ability andcapacity to drink wine. (p. 95)

Later fictionists like Ninotcha Rosca also writes political satire works reflectingPhilippine-U.S. relations during the Marcos era. Her first novels, *State of War* in 1988 and *Twice Blessed* in 1992, are both concerned with the experience of the Marcos era and the martial law period.

Another expatriate writer, Jessica Hagedorn is said to have been influenced by Carlos Bulosan.Hagedorn is a Filipina and now an American playwright, poet, and multimedia performance artist. Her first novel, *Dogeaters* published in 1990, illuminates several various aspects of Filipino experience with emphasis on the American influence through media such as radio, television, and movies. Her book, *Danger and Beauty* published in 2002, includes the satiricalnovella *Pet Food*. It muses about love and sex—probes with wry humor and social satire, the heart and heartbreaks of the immigrant experience. Her other work, *Dream Jungle* published in 2003, is described by The novel *Dream Jungle* published in 2003portrays the Philippines asa nation in crisis with traces of colonialism legacy, class struggles, family relationships, and responsibilities.

In a similar manner, Miguel Syjuco's *Ilustrado,* published in 2010, and exposes the country's search for identity over 150 years of history. As a freelance Filipino writer based in America, Syjuco's novel uses a female protagonist's colorful rise to the top of a fictional society. Through satire and parody, he examines his own biases, justifications, and limitationsas a male writer to better understand gender politics in developing societies.

It can be deemed that most of the expatriate writers from the time of Rizal to Bienvenido Santos, Carlos Bulosan, Alejandro Roces, Ninotcha Rosca and contemporary novelists, such as Merlinda Bobis, Jessica Hagedorn, and Miguel Syjuco use satire through nostalgic approachin their works.

CONCLUSIONS AND RECOMMENDATIONS

There are obvious traces of satire that are manifested in the works of Filipinos from theearly novels during the Spanish regime, novels in English during the American period, and novels by expatriate writers. The latter uses satire concealed behind the nostalgic accounts oftheir home country. Their creative works serve as an outflow of emotions that long for their own identity as Filipinos by heart and at the same time discover the ills and flaws of the society.Although different in their individual style, common factors, such as the traces of custombrismo and societal problems, can be easily identified. Their crafts, as Hornedo calls it,signify language in conveying lived experience. Accordingly, "literature tells by the use of words and idiomatic tropes and descriptions/narratives calculated to recall to perception memories or traces of lived experience."

Based on the satirical techniques and devices in the novels, the researcher regrouped those that can be called Filipino satire. The novels are filled with examples of ridiculous ideasand instances that suggest distinct Filipinos' initial source of humor. Said instances after the initial laugh will invoke thinking for a possible remedy to the object, person, or idea being ridiculed. Such problems are rooted in culture and inherent to their local ways of life.

It is therefore suggested to consider Filipino satire in understanding our culture since they are culture-bound and culture-based. Satire can be a good vehicle of how a work of fiction can provide criticisms of the society through its aesthetics.

ACKNOWLEDGEMENT

This paper was supported by the Sorsogon State University (SSU) and research funds wereprovided by the Commission on Higher Education (CHED).

ENDNOTES

[i] Merlinda Bobis. *Banana Heart Summer*. (Pasig City, Philippines: Anvil Publishing Inc.,2005); *The SolemnLantern Maker*. (USA: Delta Trade Paperbacks, 2009); *Fish-hair Woman*. (Manila, Philippines: Anvil Publishing Inc., 2012).

[ii] Florentino H. Hornedo. *Ideas and ideals: Essays in Filipino Cognitive History*. (Manila, Philippines: USTPublishing house, 2001), p.124.

[iii] Resil Mojares. *Origins and Rise of the Filipino Novel. A Generic Study of the Novel Until 1940* (QuezonCity, Philippines: UP Press, 1983), p.55.

[iv] Compiled in the book, *The Philippine Novel in English. Galdon J. , ed.*(Quezon City, Philippines: Ateneo DeManila University Press, 1979) p. 73

[v] A Filipino-Australian writer, who publishes in three languages across multiple genres and writes about other socio-political problems such as child abuse, migrant workers, poverty in the countryside, militarization, political detainees and imperialism.

[vi] F.H.Hornedo, . *Culture and community in the Philippine Fiesta and Other Celebrations* (Manila, Philippines: UST Publishing House, 2000)p. 51. The article is originally a lecture given at the Institute of Philippine Literature, Ateneo De Manila University in Summer 1978.

[vii] Bicolanos are the residents of Region V in the Philippines known as Bicol. It is the southern part of Luzon, the biggest island of the country.

[viii] Rice cooked too soon is a Filipino idiomatic expression referring to an early marriage.

[ix] That come out of the armpit , another Filipino idiomatic expression which means coming from nowhere orsudden arrival of the baby.

[x] Tongue eaten by the devil means being silent at all circumstances.

[xi] M.B. Sy. *Humor in Alejandro Roces' Fiction*. IAMURE International Journal of Literature, Philosophy andReligion. 4, (June 2013), p. 89

REFERENCES

Abrams, M.H. (1999). *A Glossary of Literary Terms:* 7th ed. Cornell: Cornell University Press.

Bobis, M. (2005). *Banana heart summer.* Pasig City, Philippines: Anvil Publishing Inc.

Bobis, M. (2009). *The Solemn Lantern Maker.* (USA: Delta Trade Paperbacks, 2009)
Bobis, M. (2012). *Fish-hair Woman.* (Manila, Philippines: Anvil Publishing Inc., 2012)

Colon, S. (2010). *General Sociology: A Simplified Approach, Revised ed.* Mandaluyong City, Philippines:National Book Store.

Galdon, J. (1985). Nostalgia and the Filipina writer. *Philippine Studies,* 33 (1), 96-105.

Galdon,J. ed. (1979) *The Philippine Novel in English.* Quezon City, Philippines: Ateneo De Manila UniversityPress.

Hornedo, F.H. (2004). *Literatura, Guro, Bansa: Mga Kuwadrong Konseptwal para sa Pagtuturo ng Literaturaat Ilang Panayam Tungkol sa Kalinagan at Wika.* Manila, Philippines: UST Publishing House.

Hornedo, F.H. (2001). *Ideas and ideals: Essays in Filipino Cognitive History.* Manila, Philippines: UST Publishing house.

Hornedo,F.H. (2000) *Culture and community in the Philippine Fiesta and Other Celebrations* (Manila,Philippines: UST Publishing House.

Lumbera, B. (1997). *Revaluation 1997: Essays on Philippine Literature, Cinema & Popular Culture.* Manila, Philippines: UST Publishing House.

Makaryk, I.R. (1993). *Encyclopedia of Contemporary Literary Theory. Approaches, Scholars, Terms* in p.144London: University of Toronto Press.

Meyer, J.C.(2000) Humor as Double-edged Sword: Four Functions of Humor in Communication, *Communication Theory*, 10 (3), 310-331.

Mojares, R. (1983). *Origins and Rise of the Filipino Novel. A Generic Study of the Novel Until 1940* QuezonCity, Philippines: UP Press

Mulder. M.P.(2002). *Humour Research: State of the Art.* available in http://purl.utwente.nl/publications/63066.

2

Food for Love: Bicolano's Culture in Merlinda Bobis' Novel

Published in IAMURE Multidisciplinary Vol. 6 June 2014
Print ISSN 2244-1530 • Online ISSN 2244-1549
doi: http://dx.doi.org/10.7718/iamure.ijlpr.v6i1.850

ABSTRACT

Food satisfies hunger and hunger obeys desire. Accordingly, desire and longing result in societal problems. Food and love may be extreme needs of humans, but the fulfillment of a human's wants through food and love may help ease such societal problems. This paper aims to unravel the culture of the Bicolanos as the theme highlighted in Merlinda Bobis' Banana Heart Summer. As a contemporary novel, Banana Heart Summer depicts the material and nonmaterial culture of Region V known as the Bicol Region. The paper presents an analysis of the novel's creative representation of food towards characters and their relationships with one another. The researcher employed Freud and Lacan'spsychoanalyzes particularly on the pleasure and reality principles. Likewise,the cultural and gender studies and semiotics are applied in the treatment of material. This descriptive-qualitative type of analysis employed on the novel highlights how cultural-domestic issues and socio-political problems brought along by poverty for food and love can be triumphed over through strong family bonds, religion-induced faith, culture-bound tradition, and palatable dishes on the table. The entire novel suggests hope and positivity amidst the evident "hunger". It offers awareness of the different types of hunger brought along by the socio-historical and political issues. The understanding of one's culture provides a better view of the world; this worldview may help identify the locale's distinctiveness.

Keywords: *Literature, Bicolanos material and nonmaterial culture, socio-historical and political issues, descriptive- qualitative analysis, semiotics, cultural and gender studies, Philippines*

INTRODUCTION

Every living thing has different needs. These needs may result from hunger, which is an indispensable act of desire and longing, be it material, cultural, or spiritual. Food can be likened to love as the former plays a crucial role in the development of every person that may result to good human relationship. In a deeper sense, desire and longing can result in societal problems; this implies that most social problems can be traced at home, where such wants of food and love are not meet. Therefore, the fulfillment of humans' wants, or needs (to make them appear important), can eventually help solve such problems.

The Philippine novel in English, as described by Galdon (1974), "has developed from early experiments with theme and technique in a borrowed language to the relative sophistication of form and content in a language that has become native, at least for the authors who have chosen to write it".He also identifies nostalgia as one of the more frequent themes for contemporary Philippine writers in English. He emphasizes that there is often in the Philippine writing the idyllic nostalgiaof longing for a home in the provinces which may either be gentle or bitterlysatiric.According to Lumbera (1997), to read a literary work, one must engagewith its language as the social practice of individuals, groups and institutions."In the article of Colayco (1977) published in Unitas, she referred to the modernnovel "that has come to mean more than a story unfolded to give pleasure to the reader. The average modern novel of today has come to be a novel with apurpose". She further explained that fiction is employed to vivify history whereinsocial concepts and objectives seem more attractive in fictional form. She quotedDaiches, "the novel has become a type of exposition, a way of putting across factsor exhortations or diagnosis and simply that". Thus, it points out that fiction isused by writers as a medium for communicating and disseminating anything and everything.

This goes to show that the novel may serve as a good source of material for oneto understand his or her identity by identifying himself or herself in the culturethat he or she practices. As a genre under fiction that developed much later thanmost oral forms of literature, the novel and other prose narratives most likelyserve the same function as the epic does in bringing to light a particular culture.

In his article entitled "*Handiong: An Original Poem by Fr. Bernardino Melendreras , OFM,*" Hornedo (2000) states that, *Ibalong*, is not an epic but oneof the poems in *Antologia Poetica,* a collection of 54 poems which includes thoseleft by Fr. Bernardino Melendreras. He was Franciscan priest assigned in theBicol region for more than two decades during the Spanish period. Hornedo's essay was first published in 1984 in Philippine Studies. The *antologia* is describedby Hornedo as a "typescript, on 32x22 cm. paper, 98 leaves of poetry (text ononly one side), and seven of notes and a brief introduction by Fr. Pastrana–Riol.

Bicol scholar, Maria Lilia Realubit, who was awarded in 2007 for her intensive study of *Ibalong* wrote an article emphasizing her renunciation of *Ibalong* as a Bicol epic. To quote Realubit from her on-line article in B*icolmail* dated September 12, 2013:

> The "Ibalon" is not a Bikol folk epic. It is written in Spanish by a Spanish missionary Rev. Fr. Bernardino Melendreras, O.F.M., who was in Bombon, Quipayo, and Libmanan in Camarines Sur and Guinobatan, Albay from 1841-1867 and learned to speak and write in Bikol.

The 1987 Philippine Constitution provides strong adherence to the study ofculture and implore its preservation, for the purpose of identity. Specifically, the charter's Article 14, sections 14 to 18, titled Arts and Culture, emphasize the nation's recognition of the importance of culture. Specifically, the two paragraphsunder section 18 highlight the support of the government to the researches of artsand culture.

> Section 18 (2). The state shall encourage and support researches and studies on the arts and culture.

The locale of this paper is the Bicol region or Bicolandia, which is one of the 17regions of the Philippines. It consists of six provinces, namely Albay, CamarinesNorte, Camarines Sur, Catanduanes, Masbate, and Sorsogon.

One of the major industries of the region is the *abaca*, sometimes referred as *Bicol hemp* is widely grown in Sorsogon, Albay, and Camarines Sur. Besides abaca, Bicol also grows coconuts and *pili*. In addition to these plants endemic to the region, the area is also known for dishes cooked in coconut milk or garnishedwith small pepper— these two ingredients are often associated to the region.

In Bobis' work, the origin of the famous dish Bicol Express is also explained. It is that when the mouth and the tongue react to the chilli, the diner shall rush to the tap for relief as fast as the Bicol Express, which is the name tagged to a couch of the Philippine National Railways that plied the Manila-Legazpi route then. In addition to that, the novel also presents an image of Mayon Volcano, alongside the ruins of the Cagsawa church which was badly damaged and partially buried during the volcano's most destructive eruption on February 1, 1814. Being so, the volcano also provides a connotative picture of the region. A record of its eruption in the summer of 1968 seems an implicit detail in the novel.

Bicolanos carry strong beliefs in religion, close family ties, and the idea of putting up with the harsh environment and weather disturbances that have molded the Bicolano's strong spirit. In the case of the novel, it is set in Remedios Street, which serves as a microcosm of a world in which both hunger and want concur with wealth. However, the presence of the church comforts people from the constant threat of the volcano. As Hefner (2006) describes the setting, Remedios Street is just a small street in the Philippines, but the smallness could be magnified as it may represent larger 'communities of hunger'.

Understanding one's culture provides a better view of the world. Culture and philosophy also go hand in hand since culture is recognized as a philosophical theme. Accordingly, philosophy lies in the ideational part of culture; thus language and behavior reflect the people's worldview.

Moreover, Hornedo (2004) wrote that "a piece of literature documents the world and the worldview of its author." It is for this reason that the researcher hopes that the findings of this study may be beneficial as a source of information specifically on the culture of the Bicolanos. Educators may also get some material from this study in uncovering Bicol identity and ideology in relation to Filipino culture in general.

This study may also help the Bicolanos/Filipinos to appreciate their cultural heritage and identity through a "repackaged" contemporary function of fiction leading to their insights in understanding themselves. It may also benefit those in the field of research, particularly in the areas of Philippine studies and different branches of the humanities.

Framework

This paper employed Abrams (1953) literary theories on the relationships between the text and the universe (mimetic); the text and the writer (expressive); the text and the reader/critique (pragmatic) and his/her close reading of the text(objective). The mimetic and pragmatic see literature with a purpose and the critic's job is to identify whether the aim of the work was achieved. The expressive and objective see literature as something to be appreciated, contemplated andobserved where the critic's task is to examine it according to its own terms asestablished by the work itself.

According to Goldstein (1964), "every society creates its own culture and literature". The same idea holds true to Dickinson (1959) who stated that a literary work is a product of its time and place. The importance of culture and literature is supported by Hornedo (1997) who claims that "culture is a life – sustaining element of society, and when elements of culture are removed without adequate replacement, society fails to cope and eventually, it breaks down". If oneis familiar with his literature, he also has knowledge of the culture incorporated in it. Thus, the study of culture and literature proves to be beneficial if one wantsto know the background of a particular society.

According to Maramba (1971) "man's culture is reflected in his literaturethat comes in varied forms". Dickinson (1959) discuss the idea of Aristotle that fiction deals with universals and it resembles philosophy which in particular also resembles history. In the local setting, Borres (1999) recommended in her study that the government and the schools should encourage and support the production, retrieval, and preservation of Bicol literary materials, and use them in establishing their relevance to contemporary life. The true meaning and significance of the novel, according to Colayco (1957) "is derived from the suggestions and cumulative views evolved from symbolism and adjustment, and enrichment of meaning at all points through style, pattern, plot, tone and every element that enters the makeup of a novel."

Likewise, Hornedo (2004) in his book, *Literatura, Guro, Bansa* (2004) introduces the use of four reality frames in teaching literature. These reality frames include literature as theme, literature as aesthetic creation, literature as script, and literature as a work of history. Given this framework, this paper's material, the novel, can be considered for analysis since it has theme, an aesthetic creation with script, and is based from history.

The novel under study was analyzed, according to structure, theme, language and local color. The use of food as a trope was utilized to trace the cultural and socio-political journey of the place that the present generation should get to know and understand. Likewise, the worldview from the deciphered societal problems was discussed to reveal the community identity. Such identity aims to promote socio-historical and cultural awareness and concern.

This paper, which analyzes a contemporary novel by someone who settled in the locality of the material's setting, can provide not only cultural information but also such details pertaining to actual social and political circumstances. In the absence of an authentic oral tradition that serves as reference of people's cultural identity, this novel—being a work of fiction—may be considered to fill the gap resulting from that absence.

Objectives of the Study

This paper aims to unravel the images of the region and its people as depicted in Bobis' contemporary novel, *Banana Heart Summer*. The paper also attempts to transcode food and culture to reveal the Bicolano's culture. Specifically, this paper sought to identify the main theme of the novel in terms of characters' representation and food signification, trace the socio-political and cultural journey of the place, and provide a source material on Bicol culture as manifested in a contemporary work of fiction.

METHODOLOGY

The creative representation of food towards the narrative's characters and relationships that suggest signification was used to delve on some issues thereby revealing the themes of the material.

This study is a descriptive-qualitative research which used formalist- contextual analysis as method. It involves documentary and content analysis validated through unstructured interviews. The documentary and content analysis focused on the creative representation of food to the narrative's characters and relationships.

In this paper, the researcher considered the use of cultural and gender studies as well as semiotics. Bressler (1999) mentions that one of the four areas of investigation in gynocritism of Showalter is culture. It is said that "by analyzing cultural forces (such as the importance and value of women's roles in a given society), critics who emphasize this area of study investigate how society shapes a woman's understanding of herself, her society and her world". Semiotics was used in discerning the food signification employed as trope in Bobis' work.

In addition, Freud's psychoanalytic theory on the pleasure and reality principles was utilized in the analysis of the characters' representation. Likewise, Lacan's idea of the unconscious that "there is a direct connection between the repressive character of language and culture and the coming into being of theunconscious" was also be considered.

This paper also deal on the use of semiotics or the signification of the novel'stext to discuss the culture of the region. Culture, as applied in this paper, is theresult of the Bicol experience. Bicolandia is a composition of three sections; each has a distinct cultural and language distinction. The Tagalog speakers are influenced by the nearby Quezon province, those from the southern provinces of Masbate and Sorsogon speak a language with Cebuano, Samarnon, or Hiligaynonadmixture and; at the heart of the region, the two cities of Naga and Legazpi, the language used is that which tacitly recognized as the "standard" Bicol.

RESULTS AND DISCUSSIONS

Author's Background

Merlinda Bobis is a multi-awarded contemporary writer from the Bicol region. She was born in then town of Tabaco, in the first district of Albay, on 25 November 1959. She is considered as the youngest of the region's new *balyanas or* writers as described by Santos (2003). In the same book, it was mentionedthat she expresses and exhibits her double otherness as Bikol and as Woman. In her works, she highlights the deconstruction of both the urban/rural and male/female binaries and presents further such contrasts. As a novelist, she brings the Bikol woman writer to the postmodern, post-theory era of the '90's whilekeeping aware of her roots and her gender.

Aside from being a skilled writer, Bobis is also a multi-talented artist whoreads, sings, and performs. She dances her prose and drama. This paper's material, *Banana Heart Summer*, won for her the Golden Book Award (*Gintong Aklat Award*) in 2006 and was shortlisted for the *Australian Literature Society* gold medal. It was also awarded *Best in Foreign Language in Fiction* from the *Manila Critics' Circle* that same year.

Structure

The story is told in the first-person point of view by a 40-year-old migrant worker named Nenita. Her tale is traced back at a time when she was 12 years old, in her hometown, and longing for the love of her mother. Her mother's dignity has been destroyed by her inability to feed her family that may have caused her violent rage towards Nenita. The nine-year old Nenita aims to be of worth to her family particularly to her mother by being a good cook and a food provider. It was when she heard of the myth of the banana heart and decided to get hold of it.

In the story, Nenita enumerates her townsfolk and describes each character while revealing how these characters are interrelated. In so doing, she vividly describes every dish representing each character and the manner of preparing it. Nenita's description is full of innocence of a child (e.g. how she narrated that babies come out from armpits after hearing her parents gasping for air from the vent). Such can be discerned from the following excerpts:

> - *to hold her tightly at night, whispering over and over again, Ilove you Maring, I love you. Then a baby always arrived from the armpit (Bobis, .71)*
> - *which clung to the waist of our father who clung to our mother and whispered, I love you, I love you, while she kept her face turned away, breathing precious air from the vent (Bobis, 73-74)*
> -

After narrating an event, the narrator fast-forwards to present events such as when she narrates the evening that her brother suddenly got hungry after listening to the "predictable breathing" that came from the other side of the mat. Specifically, Nenita shifts to this:

> *This was a story that he would tell me years later in his*
> *weary letters, which always asked whether I could send*
> *the family's a little bit of help (Bobis, 202.)*

The same is true when the narrator talks about falling in love, her ability as a child and her misunderstanding of the difference between 'stolen and the bought taste'.

> *But how can I save that twelve-year old from these*
> *arguments? Of course I love my own? Even today, it takes*
> *great effort to believe myself (Bobis, 131).*

> *I could climb any tree at my time (Bobis, 132).*

> *That summer I was twelve, lihi made sense. Mother*
> *vented her spleen on me because she was pregnant, and*
> *she couldn't help it. Today, twenty years later, and so*
> *far away from home, I understand and I forgive*
> *(Bobis, 103).*

Language and Local Color

Another feature of the novel that points to the author's personal style and artistry is the use of local terminologies, coined from Bicol and Spanish. The words and phrases signify the people's strong religious affiliation to Catholicism, which is understandable given the colonization of the Philippines by the Spaniards. Some of these words include:

> *Ay Dios ko.*
> *Ay santisima   (p.*
> *25)*

> *Ay, por dios y por*
> *Santo Aysus (p.*
> *136)*

Other Spanish terms used in the narrative are:

Señorita   *Señora*

Amor propio   *Dispensa*

Agua de Mayo   *puñeta*

Banderitas   *Immaculada Concepcion*

There are also some expressions in the vernacular that carry another meaning. These can be considered as local idiomatic expressions which can be interpreted with reference to the culture of the region. Some of these expressions are:

> *Ay, mahamis na kalbaryo (p.*
> *116)*
> *Ay, dae lamang kinutsara (p*
> *209)*

Ay, mahamis na kalbaryo carries the literal meaning "a sweet Calvary", can easily trace its meaning to the characteristics of the two words, sweet and Calvary. Sweet refers to the sweetness of the guava fruit, which, if eaten half-ripe with a bit of salt, is crunchy and tastes sour. However, when the sweetest part is eaten ripe with the rose-pink seeds, the guava fruit itself causes constipation. The narrator explains it in the following lines:

> *Because eating the sweetest part, especially too much of it,*
> *means an agonizing internal journey in the lower regions,*
> *like that mythical descent into hell. Such is the nature of*
> *constipation most dire (p. 116).*

Calvary is a biblical place always associated with suffering since it was where the Jesus Christ the Savior was crucified. Such sacrificial act in the Roman Catholic Church is said to be the utmost showcase God's love for mankind.

Ay, dae lamang kinutsara, which means, "it was not even spooned," is explained in the narrative as an exasperated comment on passions or words allowed to run wild and easy. It is further discussed through an example of an imagined phenomenon when Nenita is still a child:

> *I imagined Father did not mind such a mess, but*
> *Mother, grim as ever, might have kept pushing a spoon*
> *at him during his own season of feverish side glances, for*
> *surely he had his own early days (p. 209).*

Other vernacular terms mentioned were present during the 60's, the time in which the novel is set. These terms are easily understood as connected to the characters' local name of food or object discussed in the narrative. For example, *marka demonyo* is a tonic drink and has an image of satanl on its label, showing him as a captive of Saint Archangel.

Another is *tiling–tiling,* which is an ice drop or an iced delicacy sold by a vendor who stirs people's attention through the sound of a bell he carries. The term *tiling-tiling* is obviously taken from the sound of the bell.

Galletas patatas and *turu-talinga* are both popular types of biscuits. Being toasted, they are hard to the bite, yet give the eater some "thrill" and would make him or her crave for more even if he or she is already full.

Lab-yu,balicucha, and *tira-tira* are all types of sweet candies that children love. *Labyu* is a chocolate made from peanuts while *both balicucha and tira-tira* have stretchable forms and are made of palm sugar and coconut milk.

Fat & thin are just salted melon seeds whose manner of eating is described in details in the narrative. The name is derived from the fat outside and the thin core.

Kudal-kudal is a local translation of the word fence. It is a town dance and may also be attributed to the idea of a man wooing his woman.

Food: Its Contextual, Socio-cultural and Role in Character's Representation

Food is ever-present throughout *Banana Heart Summer* as it plays an important cultural and psychological role in the story. Hunger is central to Nenita's world and being. Food is used as a subject-matter set against the background of love as a human emotion. Love and food—associated with "hunger"—are two sides of the same coin. The novel explores what hunger is in the social context. Hefner describes hunger as:

"Hunger we all experience. Hunger is the greatest leveler of humankind, if it wishes to be leveled. But how and whether we appease it always restores the social order".

Each of the stories begins sweetly only to be edged with bitterness towards the end of the novel. This change is not viewed entirely without sorrow but is seen as an inevitable growth as characters begin to approach understanding of their lives. For Nenita, everything has a flavor and every flavor has its purpose. Bitterness holds as much importance as its counterpart. However, it is in the mixing of the two that our deepest longings are confronted. To quote the narrator:

> *-because hunger is always unsightly. It's our gut*
> *hanging out, unkempt like unassuaged love. We see it*
> *in someone else and instinctively we grab at our*
> *stomachs, then quickly withdraw our hands, knowing we*
> *have betrayed ourselves (Bobis, 187).*

The whole novel is packed with signs and metaphors that arouse the reader's senses. Any and every mention of food is suggestive of something else, suchas the implied correlation between deep-frying the Filipino delicacy *turon* (jackfruit and plantain wrapped in a spring roll) and the sound and smell of happiness. One of the characters, *Nana Dora*, is also described similar to thejackfruit, which is "too prickly outside but sweet inside, but only if she was ripe enough to entertain your intrusions" (p.9).

The preparation of the shredded heart in coconut milk is also aptly described:

> *"It must be the right heart, it must be the soft core of the right heart, it must be the yellowish part of the soft core of the right heart" (Bobis, 10).*

Nenita has also presuppositions that the devil ate her father's tongue by cooking it in mushroom sauce, which happens to be the same way that the Spanish cooked ox tongue.

The *palitaw,* or the floated one, carry a similar impression to those who eat it,such as the floating faith of Tiya Coring, the mother ofBasilio Profundo, In the text, *palitaw* is comparatively likened to faith, such as in the following excerpt:

> *"faith always floats, keeps us afloat. As it is in swimming, so it is in cooking, so it is in falling in love. We always believe we'll riseto the surface. Faith is too light to stay down, and it smells. Wecan't hide it (Bobis, 20).*

Further, this part of the novel describes that floating faith makes us braveand endure consequences. Dignity is also explained as may be lean but morefilling than faith.

In the seventh and eighth chapters, seaweed salad and the Calcium Man with pili nut husk on the side and the chapter titled, Halo-halo:

mix-mixed intentions foretell the ideas on dignity and pride. The narrator recounts that, "mother said pride is a sin, but dignity is a savior".

Moreover, through the narrator's encounter with Manolito Ching describedas the Spanish-Chinese mestizo and the heir to the fortunes of the richest businessman in town, she confirms the bitter reality of being poor. He narrates, "The poorest are whipped by the poor, and the poor are whipped by the rich, even without them lifting a finger"(p.31). Hardly, Nenita also realizes that "culinary tricks, especially the more adventurous ones, never apply to human relationships (p. 40).

The smoky coconut chicken in green papayas is used to present the strangenessbehind an attempt to make 'better' the smell, taste, texture, or look of nature. In addition, the narrator states that the heart of the matter offends the palate, andwhen it does not offend, it scares. Thus, the text concludes, *"So we arm ourselveswith herbs and spices, and we consider ourselves improved as a species"* (p. 49). Thisis similar to how each person lives and pretends as somebody else or have a made-up identity.

The art of preserving is likened to the preparation and preservation of thetaste of *acharra*, a preserved shredded and soaked green papayas in vinegar. Forexample, Maria Corazon Alano is described based on the speculations of the narrator as having an experiment of her new version of preserving domestic harmony. The text reads:

> *When in her heart, a wife decides that she's no longer one, notby her husband's decree or imputation, then she becomes playful. Without leaving, she can be single again, a maiden, a girl. The sense of old self can be recovered and preserved, where it had been adultered or diminished (Bobis, 218).*

The strange synthesis of cookery, tales, and of human interaction is the dominant metaphorical theme of the novel, which, categorically speaking, appeals more to the intellect rather than to the senses. This appeal can be discerned amid the strewn metaphors that frequently appear in the novel.

The novel also attempts to establish a literary continuity between food preparation, consumption, and human relations. It aims to present the facets of human relationships that can be explained creatively and understood in termsof food.

Local Myths, Legends, and other Practices related with Food

Merlinda Bobis connects the readers into the world of the young, innocent,yet responsible protagonist, Nenita/Nining. Bobis uses the elements of the sensesand imparts the rich idea of the place, characters, and culture to the reader. The sights, sounds, and smells are translated and captured into a particular taste in the narrative embedded with metaphors. The style then encourages the readersto understand relationships between and among people like the blending of ingredients in a recipe.

Nenita's love for luscious meals reflects her desire for a fulfilling and happy life that was deprived of her on her younger days. Bobis has portrayed this desirethrough the nostalgic elements in her manner of narrating Nenita's childhood through the known beliefs and practices of the narrator. In addition to the novel's artistic value, food is used to present the author's hometown and localmyths and practices.

The Myth of the Banana Heart

> *Close to midnight when the heart bows from its stem,*
> *wait for its first dew. It will drop like a gem. Catch it*

with your tongue. When you eat the heart of the matter,
you'll never grow hungry again (p.2)

In the novel, the preceding myth is told by Nana Dora, the old woman whohad no children and who cooked the best and cheapest snacks on Remedios Street. Nana Dora tells the myth to the narrator at the beginning of the narrative. Hearing the myth from an old woman, Nining or Nenita eventually believes that the lesson the myth intends to impart is indeed true.

The story takes place during summer. It is then when the narrator states, "sheate the heart of the matter." The statement may have various interpretations (e.g. the summer when Nining was able to catch the banana heart that would haveappeased her hunger as well as her family's). It could be assumed that Nenita did it for curiosity, innocence, or out of desperation to satisfy desire or want. Shemight have waited for "the dew" from the stem of a banana heart one midnight. Since the heart has a pointed shape which lowers at night due to accumulatedfog, this could have been assumed as 'the heart of the matter".

In a deeper understanding, "eating the heart of the matter" may refer to how the protagonist fulfills the family's needs that the parents cannot provide when she was young. By being the domestic helper of Miss VV's family, Nenita put food on her family's table. This may strengthen the idea behind the myth since that job helped her to acquire a lifetime source of income.

The Legend of the Bittermelon

This legend is told when the narrator injures her back and when she describesBoy Hapon's' fringe garden. In a way, using the idea behind the legend, it could resemble the story of Nenita's mother. Nenita's mother's being harsh on Nenita might be understood as her rage over the situation she was trapped in. Maring,her mother, is described idiomatically as "rice cooked too soon".

The story of Maring tells that she was once a sweet school girl, who fell in love with and married a mason. It was because of that that her family—the so- called "rich relations," eventually despised her. When Nenita and Junior were her only children, that was the time when she could still laugh. As the number of children increased, her bad temper grew. The narrator describes her as:

> *Want is bitter, graceless. It disparages those who have the power to appease it in themselves. The underbelly of unappeased want is even worse. Envy is twice bitter, and bitterness is an acquired taste (p. 82).*

The Myth of *Lihi*

> *A pregnant woman can irrationally like or dislike someone or something, which is the object of her "lihi". This dislike can be extreme, mercilessly splenic. Like, on the other hand, can be almost amorous. Usually, it is an excessive desire of the palate for mostly sour things. She must have them even if you have to steal them (p. 102.)*

That a pregnant woman craves for different things is a known fact. In the narrative, since Nenita attempts to win her mother's affection, she steals some mangoes and accidentally falls from the tree but is luckily saved by Boy Hapon. Such experiences are narrated by a narrator who knows that *lihi* is not associated with Nenita's mother's rage Nenita herself.

To quote the narrator's words, "today, twenty years later and so far away from home, I understand and I forgive" (p. 103). This may mean that the reality behind the rage is still the sad fact about Maring's shame and sorrow over what happened to her. The narrative states that shame *comes from wanting, and it is thirsty while sorrow is runny, always painfully wet* (p.68). The hormonal imbalance caused by pregnancy plus the idea of having another mouth to feed despite the family's poverty could have brought the rage that is disguised as *lihi*.

Other Beliefs
o several other beliefs

> **4.1.** *Pag nagkaon ka ki odo kang saday, matitipsikan ka- maturon iyan (p.91). Translation: If you ate feces when you were a baby, you're bound to get burned by hot oil when you grow up.*

> **4.2** *A baby who sucks his toes means his mother will soon be pregnant again (p.92).*

> **4.3** *Tales of securing the chilli pants first, before the house, whenever there was a storm (p. 141).*

> **4.4.** *If the husband leaves the house after a quarrel, the wife should hang his shirt over the stove and whip it several times (p. 195).*

There are other thematic aspects concealed in *Banana Heart Summer*, although, it appears as a stimulating food novel. The novel features a moving story and articulates the language of food. This language supports the novel in reaffirming the passion and perseverance of the Filipino, particularly the Bicolanos, in facing life's many challenges.

Societal Problems

The critical reader can identify some societal problems in the novel and may realize that these are primarily caused by material and spiritual hunger. These problems include child abuse, child labor, corruption, illicit affair, local and overseas employment resulting from the absence of work in the Philippines.

Child abuse is evident in various situations all throughout the novel and in the life of Nening. Her mother punishes and beats her even for a trivial mistake, usually associated with food. Though Nenita is not forced to work as a housemaid, there is no instance that the parents are opposed to the idea; in fact, they eventually relied on their daughter's support.

Employment problems can be seen as the primary source of poverty among the characters in the novel. It eventually results in domino effect that can be both positive and negative as in the case of Gable and the suicide of Tio Anding. The father of Nening shows his lame machismo attitude by having children though he has no stable means of supporting them. Consequently, the whole family suffers from poverty. Similarly, Tio Anding's family is the poorest in the neighborhood. His desperation when he loses the job in the midst of crisiscoupled with an ill wife and starving twins pushed him to end his life. The positive points can be drawn during the wake when everybody is described asgenerous for sharing every available resource to the bereaved family. In the case of Gable, he seems extra romantic every time Maring is pregnant with anotherbaby.

Corruption is manifested the town mayor, Mr. Ching, the politician character. The novel presents the issue of corruption as being natural and rampant during periods of crisis when aids from other countries abound in thelocale. Mr. Ching's corruptive nature is implied when he takes the crisis as anopportunity to become richer. His character is radiated towards the corrupt official, the town mayor, who is not a pure native Filipino but a Chinese nationalconsidered as the richest in the narrator's village.

Morality-wise, the novel presents another problem. This is seen in pregnancyout of wedlock, which is certainly a perpetual problem. To solve this problemin the context of the novel, Ms. VV is hastily married to a "generous" personwho is willing to save someone from people's harsh mouths. The pregnancy of Ms.VV and her engagement to another man who is old enough to be her father is presented through folk aphorisms, that is, by using terms such as *immaculada concepcion* and *Joseph*. Her affair with Mr. Gusting Alano eventually bears another unexpected problem, the solution to which paved the way to Nenita's being the first and the youngest domestic helper from their village. This situation in the novel can be viewed either positively or negatively depending on the perspective of the reader. When Nenita's parents allow Nenita to work abroad along with her mistress, Ms. VV, the decision totally closes the door of opportunity for Nenita to continue with her studies. On the other hand, it may also be another way for Nenita to explore and widen her horizon although it limits her opportunity to study and work despite her young age.

CONCLUSIONS

In the book, material poverty coexists alongside spiritual poverty. The former functions as a dual role that fuels Nenita's endless pursuit of maternal love. The novel depicts an aching need for acceptance and love in the lives of those who live on Remedios Street during that summer. The dramas of other characters' relationship and love help the narrator struggles to satisfy her need to establish a relationship with her abusive mother. Most characters are semi-pathetic individuals eternally searching for inner peace.

The nourishment of body and soul is the most sought idea in the novel. The narrator and other characters long for satisfaction and fulfillment of their desires. Nenita's longing for the maternal love of Maring is her motivation to seek for a local and eventually foreign employment at a young age. Maring's yearning for the acceptance of her parents and society for marrying a mason is seen through her personal idea of dignity and pride. Miss VV's decision to marry a man old enough to be her father could represent a refuge for the love that she could never have. Nana Dora's beliefs in myths could be attributed to her desires such as her husband's coming home.

The use of food in the novel and the title itself, suggests *hybridity* or *nativization*; by such terms, characters perform or do things based from their needs. They adapt themselves according to what could help them fulfil their wants. Female is also labeled as the one who prepares food and responsible for harmony at home. The female's love leads to heroism owing to their intention to help their loved ones and themselves. Hence, the entire novel suggests hope and positivity amid the underlying problems related to "hunger".

The Bicolanos' culture, therefore, is a juxtaposition of the universal idea of love and belongingness. Humankind aims to satisfy one's need amid the difficulty and risk in the process. The said worldview of love and belongingness also deals with the issue of human relationship rooted from the home topped with inherent desire of acceptance and being a worthy individual in the society. Hence, Bicolanos are Filipinos who believe in the idea of faith, courage and optimism despite the inevitable natural and environmental factors, as well as problems caused by human intervention.

RECOMMENDATIONS

The researcher would like to recommend the inclusion of contemporary novel/s in teaching Philippine literature particularly regional literature. The application of the four reality frames in teaching literature is also encouraged.

LITERATURE CITED

Abrams, M. H. (1953). *The mirror and the lamp:* Romantic theory and the critical tradition. Oxford: Oxford University Press Inc.

Bobis, M. (2008). *Banana Heart Summer*. Random House LLC. Retrieved onMay 15, 2013 from http://goo.gl/QqXJUq

Borres, MJ. (1999). Cantata of the Warrior Woman, A Bikol Epic Written by Merlinda C. Bobis: An Analysis.Retrieved on September 29, 2013 from http://goo.gl/ips8XO

Colayco, C. (1957). *The Novelist: A Portrait Painter*. Unitas, UST, Manila, 30, (4), 840-848.

Congress of the Philippines (1987). Philippine Constitution. Retrieved on June20, 2013 from http://goo.gl/ePhP1L

Dickinson, L. (1959). A Guide to Literary Study. University of Missouri: USA. Retrieved on September 29, 2013 from http://goo.gl/mqnLXr

Galdon, J.A. (1979). *Essays on the Philippine novel in English/edited by Joseph A. Galdon.* Ateneo de Manila University Press. Retrieved on June 19, 2013fromhttp://goo.gl/HPKnkv

Goldstein, K. (1964). *A guide for field workers in folklore* (Vol. 52). Gale/Cengage Learning. Retrieved on September 29, 2013 from http://goo.gl/V90aTq

Hefner, R. (2006). Balancing Heart and Spleen. Eureka Street. Retrieved on June20, 2013 from http://goo.gl/CHJfuf

Hornedo, F. (1997). *Pagmamahal and Pagmumura: Essays.* Office.. Retrieved on September 29, 2013 from http://goo.gl/E1G4EZ

Hornedo, F. H. (2004). *Literatura, guro, bansa: mga kuwadrong konseptwal para sa pagtuturo ng literatura at ilang panayam tungkol sa kalinangan at wika.* USTPublishing House. Retrieved onJune 25, 2013 from http://goo.gl/iUO8Hi

Hornedo, F. H. (2000). *Culture and Community in the Philippine Fiesta and otherCelebrations.* University of Santo Tomas Pub. House. Retrieved on June 25,2013 from http://goo.gl/XpkpgN

Hornedo, F.H. (1984) Philippine Studies, 32(4), 526–528. Retrieved on July 18,
2013 from http://goo.gl/vmP5PE

Lévi-Strauss, C., & O'Flaherty, W. D. (1979) *Myth and meaning* (pp. 34-43).New York: Schocken Books. Retrieved on June 20, 2013 from http://goo.gl/Teomqb

Lucero, R. C. (2007). *Ang Bayan Sa Labas Ng Maynila*. Ateneo University Press.

Retrieved on July 19, 2013 from http://goo.gl/ZA7WQJ

Lumbera, B. (1997). Revaluation 1997: Essays on Philippine Literature, Cinema and Popular Culture. *Manila: University of Santo Tomas Publishing House*. Retrieved on June 20, 2013 from http://goo.gl/LWVjIJ

Maramba, A.D. (1971). *Early Philippine literature from ancient times to 1940: with teaching notes and study guides*. Published and exclusively distributed by Anvil.. Retrieved on September 29, 2013 from http://goo.gl/iN5622

Santos, P. V. M. (2003). *Hagkus: Twentieth-century Bikol women writers*. De LaSalle University Press. Retrieved on July 18, 2013 from http://goo.gl/Qqfmjk

3

Satire in Merlinda Bobis' *Banana Heart Summer*

Published in JPAIR Multidisciplinary Research Vol. 19 · January 2015
Print ISSN 2012-3981 • Online ISSN 2244-0445
doi: http://dx.doi.org/10.7719/jpair.v19i1.309

ABSTRACT

Hornedo, a literature icon asserts that "A piece of literature documents the world and the worldview of its author." Accordingly, some literary pieces can provide information on the socio-political and cultural background of a certain society. Anchored on this premise, this paper aimed to identify the aesthetics of satire in Merlinda Bobis' Banana Heart Summer. It also sought to unveil the novel's message and the author's manner of criticizing the novel's social setup. Specifically, it sought to describe the novel's theme, tone, structure and style, as well as the socio-political and cultural aspects using food as primary trope. The paper also aimed to present the reality frame of the depicted societal problems of the Filipinos in general and those of Bicolanos in particular. The formalist theory was applied in the treatment of material, which is a satire, and being so, the researcher also applied defamiliarization theory, through devices such as tropes and social realism, as it forms part of the aesthetics of satire that can help identify the ideology behind the author's work. The researcher grouped the identified satirical techniques into five: exaggeration, incongruity, parody, reversal, and defamiliarization. In conclusion, this paper asserts that Bobis wrote the material for the readers to see the flaws of the society; alongside, she also implicitly offers a solution or presents the possibility of curing the social ills highlighted in the novel

Keywords: *Literature, aesthetics of satire, defamiliarization, Banana heart summer, Bicolanos, Filipinos, formalist-contextual analysis, Philippines.*

INTRODUCTION

In her *Hagkus* Twentieth-century Bikol Women Writers (2003:149), Paz Verdades M. Santos describes Merlinda Carullo Bobis as "the most prolific, most awarded, and most skilled of all the Bikol women writers and the youngest of the region's new *balyanas or* female writers". In some of her works, Bobis, who was born in what is now the City of Tabaco, in the first district of Albay, on November 25, 1959, she expresses and exhibits her double otherness as Bikol and as Woman. She also highlights the deconstruction of both the urban/rural and male/female binaries and presents further such contrasts. Santos further describes Bobis as:

> *As a novelist, she brings the Bikol woman writer to the postmodern, post-theory era of the '90's while keeping aware of her roots and of her gender.* (p.148)

Besides writing, Bobis also paints, reads, sings, and performs. She sings and dances her prose and drama; in fact, she has performed in Australia, Philippines, US, Spain, France and China. As a Filipino-Australian writer, she publishes in three languages across multiple genres, with her works receiving recognition from award-giving organizations in the Philippines and abroad. Some of the various awards she has received are Prix Italia, the Steel Rudd Award for the Best Published Collection of Australian Short Stories, the Philippine National Book Award, and the Australian Writers' Guild Award.

In this paper, the researcher mapped out the Bikol writers both male and femaleand considered that among them, Bobis is a standout because of her multinationaland international awards and her works cover all genres from poetry to prose. Although the list of Bikol writers was trimmed down to those writing in English, Bobis remains significant as she writes in three languages—Bicol, Filipino, and English. Aside from such an impeccable accomplishment, Bobis is also includedin the list of Bikol writers writing both poetry and prose including play or drama. All the above-mentioned feats justify that Bobis is undoubtedly a multiawarded, multilingual writer across genres, hence, encouraging the researcher to choose Bobis and her work (the novel, in particular) as the subject of her study.

To date, Bobis has received four major awards in the Philippines for her collection of poetry. In Australia, her collection of poetry was published as *Summer Was a Fast Train without Terminals*, which was shortlisted in the PoetryBook of the Year award.

Alongside her poetry, Bobis is also into drama and play, where she has alsoproven her prowess. For example, her one-act play, *Ms. Serena Serenata* was recognized by the Carlos Palanca Awards Committee. In addition, *Rita's Lullaby*, a radio drama, received three awards in Australia such as Ian Reed Foundation Prize, Australian Writer's Guild Award and Prix Italia or international award. Bobis' epic poem, (*Daragang Magayon, Cantata*) was also named finalist in The Australian Classical Music award.

Equally outstanding are Bobis' fictional works which have also garnered various awards since 1997, having received 12 awards for her short stories and novels, each with six awards. These short stories and novels were published whenshe was already working in Australia as a creative writing professor in Wollongong University where she also had a scholarship to pursue her doctorate degreein Creative Writing. It was after her eleven years of teaching in the different institutions in the Philippines. On the third year of her doctorate program, she applied for a teaching job at Wollongong University, where she is still working asa creative writing professor.

Two of her novels, *Banana Heart Summer* and *Fish-Hair Woman* are explicitly and implicitly set in the rural areas of the Bikol region, Remedios Street and Iraya. Bicol or Bicolandia, is one of the 17 regions of the Philippines; it consists six provinces, namely Albay, Camarines Norte, Camarines Sur, Catanduanes, Masbate, and Sorsogon. The other novel, *The Solemn Lantern Maker* is set inthe heart of Metro Manila, an urban area. The settings of these novels providenot only cultural information but also actual social and political circumstances, which prove relevant to the plot structure.

The first of the three novels, *Banana Heart Summer*, suggests a bright scene and light tone yet filled with latent meanings. The whole novel is packed withsigns and metaphors that stir the reader's senses. For example, the novel explicitly mentions food, but one reading it critically could explore on the suggestive meaning of these details. Bobis skillfully and purposefully weaves cookery with such sequence of events in the neighborhood among the townsfolk.

The Solemn Lantern Maker and *Fish-Hair* Woman, manifest the same level of Bobis' craftsmanship; however, both works are of darker color and serioustones, revealing serious societal issues such as child prostitution, militarization, total war, urban poverty, and political connivance of the Philippines with othercountries.

Bobis' themes in her novels and this paper's material reflect the major problem of poverty. It is also the main concern of the Association of Southeast Asian Nations (ASEAN). This regional grouping aims to alleviate the problemof poverty in particular. The Extreme Poverty Conference held in Bangkok in April 2015, assembled global and regional intellectuals to confer about the latest issues on poverty in Asia. The keynote speaker Stephen O'Connell, USAID's Chief Economist discusses the conference' objective which is "to improve the well-being of the extreme poor and protect the less poor from shocks that might pull them into extreme poverty and to produce a policy briefer identifying the most efficient and sustainable approaches to improving the well-being of theextreme poor" (The Asia Foundation, 2015).

This analysis aimed to reveal Bobis' criticism particularly of the ugliness of the Filipinos' hospitality, particularly that of the Bicolanos. According to Lumbera (1997:58), reading a literary work requires one to "engage with its language as the social practice of individuals, groups and institutions." He refers to Philippine literature as that which "may be produced in the capital city of Manila and in the different urban centers and rural outposts, even in foreign land where descendantsof Filipino migrants use English or any of the languages of the Philippines to create works that tell about their lives and aspirations". This goes to show that thenovels—though written in another country and a foreign language—may stillserve as a good source of material on Philippine studies. Furthermore, Lumbera says:

The forms used by Filipino authors may be indigenous or borrowed from other cultures, and these may range from popular pieces addressed to mass audiencesto highly sophisticated works intended for the intellectual elite. (p. 2)

Indeed, novels are intended to arouse emotions by allowing readers to make intellectual discoveries of ideals creatively embedded in the writer's artistry through thematic presentation, form, style, and general structure of the work. These discoveries also lead them to decipher ideas which can enlighten, inspire orsimply inform them accordingly.

Xi Tian (2014) concludes in his study, *Uncertain Satire in Modern Chinese Fiction and Drama: 1930-1949* that the people in China may find difficulty in expressing their complaints in politics through traditional media like books and newspapers. His ideas are expressed in the following excerpts:

But the internet and satire provide them a platform to vent their grievances and receive immediate responses from others. The instability of satiricaltriangle becomes even more obvious in today's satire, which is mixed with laughter, anger, carelessness and other emotions, simultaneously blurring theboundaries between satirists and the reader and even inviting unexpected satirized objects.(183)

The above idea conforms to the objectives of this paper, which is to identify the satirical tropes used in the novel under study. *Banana Heart Summer* is aPhilippine novel written to expose the follies of the society through the techniqueof defamiliarization.

In his book Essays on The Philippine Novel in English, Galdon (1985) enumerates women writers who have played significant roles in the developmentof Philippine writing in English. In the same work, he identifies nostalgia as one of the more frequent themes of contemporary Philippine writers in English. In addition, he has observed that Philippine writing often highlights the idyllicnostalgia or longing for home in the provinces which he considers either gentle or bitterly satiric. Specifically, Lumbera defines nostalgia this way:

Nostalgia is the melancholy longing for home, or the wistful and often sentimental yearning for a real or romanticized past that cannot be regained. It is often characterized by innocence, even by naivete in ironic conjunction with manipulative cleverness, authentic simplicity and a quality of frustrated aspiration which characterizes dreamland (pp. 96-97)

It is safe to say that most of the expatriate writers from Rizal to Carlos Bulosan, Gilda Cordero Fernando, Ninotcha Rosca and the contemporary novelists suchas Jessica Hagedorn and Miguel Syjuco use satire through nostalgic approach in their writings. Abrams (1999:275) defines satire as "the literary art of diminishingor derogating a subject by making it ridiculous and evoking toward its attitudes of amusement, contempt, scorn, or indignation". Satire differs from comic since the latter evokes laughter mainly as an end in itself; a satire ridicules and uses laughter as a weapon, and against a butt that exists outside the work itself. The aesthetics of satire can be identified through the theme and tone. Furthermore, Abrams explains the aesthetics of satire in the following statements

> *Satire occurs as an incidental element within many works whose overall mode is not satiric-in a certain character or situation, or in an interpolated passage of ironic commentary on some aspect of the human condition or of contemporary society. The most common indirect form is that of a fictional narrative, in which the objects of the satire are characters who make themselves and their opinions ridiculous or obnoxious by what they think, say, and do, and are sometimes made even more ridiculous by the author's comments and narrative style. (p.277).*

Theme and tone are considered valuable factors of aesthetics. Abrams (1999:170) defines theme as the "general concept or doctrine, whether implicit or asserted, which an imaginative work is designed to incorporate and make persuasive to the reader". On the other hand, tone, according to Abrams (1999:218) by quoting I.A. Richards, is "the expression of a literary speaker's attitude to his listener". The tone of an utterance reflects the speaker's sense of how he or she stands towards his or her audience or listener and in the case of written piece, the reader.

In an article published in *Ad Veritatem* (2011), Sy-Ng concludes that by studying the novel in a Lacanian framework, the literary work is elevated from Philippine to universal culture. Specifically, Sy-Ng writes:

> *Unveiling the unconscious discourse in Banana Heart Summer allows the text's meaning to come to fullness. Through a Lacanian analysis, the reader is able to see that underneath the diversity of the characters' experiences is a shared experience of self-fortification. The Lacanian analysis of the intrinsic complexities of the psyche as it engages the realm of the interpersonal and the social brings unity*

and cohesion among seemingly dispersed elements present in the plot. (2001: 257)

The pattern of the food tropes in the novel gives the different characters and subplots interconnection. As Fernandez discusses in her article published in *Philippine Studies* (1988), Filipino food is shaped by history and society; it consists of a Malay matrix, with the melded and blended influences from China and India, Spain and America. Fernandez also cites the anthropologist Naomichi Ishige, who said "eating is the act of ingesting the environment." In her article, "What is Dietary Culture" she explains that eating is similar to ingesting culture because the most permanent traces left by foreign cultures on Philippine life is food

Sy-Ng's, Fernandez' and Ishige's articles are relevant to this paper given that they underscore food as a trope; critically, this trope can be used to analyze the material at hand. The present study also employed Freudian and Lacanian psychoanalysis in the interpretation of the material in order to decipher the signification of food and other tropes as well as the representation of the characters in the novel.

In her article, *Humor in Alejandro Roces' Fiction*, (2013) Sy points out that humor is used as a form of ridiculing Filipino vice particularly cockfight. She stresses that Filipinos are fond of gambling as a form of entertainment. Sy bases these claims on Roces' work *We Filipinos Are Mild Drinkers, Of Cocks and Hens, Of Cocks and Kings, Of cocks and Battle Cocks,* which, according to her, employs an apparently light tone that allows readers to understand the folly of the characters, making them appear amusing rather than annoying. The same thing holds true in the use of jokes, which, could be "half-meant", considering the truth that jokes are meant to convey.

In his article in *Ideals and Ideals: Essays in Filipino Cognitive History* (2001), Hornedo discusses that political jokes imply and reflect the society's aspiration. He also stresses that humor is dependent on one's culture and that jokes are embedded in culture and even history. For instance, during Marcos regime, thesubjects of ridicule were those who had power, such as The President and hisFirst Lady. The political undertones in jokes such as these manifest the Filipinos' dissatisfaction and disappointment with the Marcoses as the country's leaders during that period.

Undeniably, Filipinos are inclined to using humor as a form of defense mechanism, so they may reasonably cope with their frustrations and hardships. However, this "art" of ridiculing their follies through humor is exclusive to Filipinos themselves. *The Asian Travellers' Handbook* published by Asia Week cautions foreigners about it, saying:

> *Do laugh when Filipinos tell jokes about themselves and their country, as theyoften do, but don't reciprocate by doing the same thing for that may causenationalistic hackles*

In a nutshell, the statement asserts that we are offended when others make funof us or a family member. On a similar note, we are offended when a foreigner makes fun of our country.

Aside from jokes, Filipinos are also fond of playing with words and acronymsthat can only be understood by those familiar with the Philippine culture. An article published in Sunstar Daily on September 26, 1997 mentions some "special acronyms" such as PAL for Plane Always Late rather than Philippine Airlines andMBA for Manager by Accident instead of Masters of Business Administration. Some terms referring to Filipino street foods have peculiar reasoning for their names like "adidas" for the barbequed chicken feet which was taken from a brand of shoes; and "isol", the chicken butt, is named as "Shakespeare" for the locally pronounced word, "pu-wet" (poet).

The above-cited literature and studies strengthen the idea that a novel, at acertain point, has a particular message to tell. In the various researches and studies made on Philippine novel, nothing provides readings on the side of satirical tropesparticularly defamiliarization. In this paper, the point of contention is to identifythe message of Bobis in the *Banana Heart Summer* through the techniques anddevices of satire. In so doing, the structure, theme, tone and tropes were the subjects of analysis to reveal the presupposition that Bobis is a satirist. This is thegap that this study hopes to bridge.

FRAMEWORK

This paper employed Hornedo's (2002:42) idea that "to an extent, the artist is an artifact of culture, and what art discloses is not an individual consciousness but a narrative larger than the individual's personal narrative of himself." Hornedo's statement asserts that a piece of literature reflects the worldview of its writer,which is the result of his/her personal experiences, basically rooted from culture.As stated by Geertz (1973:448), "culture consists of the ensemble of stories we tell ourselves about ourselves". He concludes that cultural studies involve theinvestigative description and construction of the relational signifieds which lie hidden behind the signifiers that constitute our daily interactions within our societies. Thus, it is possible to affirm that culture is a rational manifestation distinctive of humans and human communities.

In addition to Hornedo's idea, Abrams (1953) literary theories on the relationships between the text and the writer (expressive) and the text and the reader/critique (pragmatic) strengthened the researcher's claim that Bobis is asatirist. The expressive theory views literature as something to be appreciated, contemplated on, and observed, in which the critic's task is to examine it according to its own terms as established by the work itself. The true meaningand significance of a novel, according to Colayco (1957) "is derived from thesuggestions and cumulative views evolved from symbolism and adjustment, and enrichment of meaning at all points through style, pattern, plot, tone and everyelement that enters the makeup of a novel."

The researcher, therefore, anchored this paper's argument on the idea thatBobis is a satirist, a Filipino expatriate writer, who also considers herself as a transnational of Australia. Her novels are reflective of how she views Philippine society in general and the Bicolanos in particular. Through the aesthetics of satire, this paper sought to disclose that Bobis writes about her society for its people to recognize the need to change and the problems that arise from the negativepatterns of behavior. Through her works, Bobis induces calls for change that may emanate from the people who may see themselves being implicitly represented by the characters in the novels.

In this paper, the researcher utilized the formalist-contextualist approach to analyze the novel's characters, theme, tone, structure, language, and local color. Abrams (1999:102) explains that Formalism is a type of literary theory and analysis which originated in Moscow and St. Petersburg in the second decade of this century. It views literature primarily as a specialized mode of language, and proposes a fundamental opposition between the literary use of language and the ordinary, "practical' use of language. The literariness of the text is thereby attained through the distinctive features of the form. Form and structure as employed in this paper refers to the principle that determines how the work is ordered andorganized.

Food in the novel is the primary trope in the defamiliarization techniques the researcher employed to identify and trace the cultural and socio-political journey of the setting of the novel. Likewise, the reality frame yielded throughthe deciphered societal problems was discussed to reveal the identity of the community in the novel. This study therefore was based on this premise.

OBJECTIVES OF THE STUDY

This paper aimed to identify the aesthetics of satire in Merlinda Bobis' novel, *Banana Heart Summer*. The researcher intended to unravel the literary devices used to reveal the themes of the stories focused on the Filipinos in general and Bicolanos in particular. Specifically, this paper sought to answer how the novel can be described in terms of characters, structure and style, theme, tone, and the use of food's representation and signification. It was also undertaken to reveal the Philippine societal problems that can be identified in the novels using the aesthetics of satire thereby revealing its socio-cultural aspects. Finally, the researcher sought to propose the Filipino and Bicolano types of satire based from the discerned reality frames of the said novel.

METHODOLOGY

This study, a descriptive-qualitative research, used the formalist-contextual analysis as method. Specifically, the method involved content analysis with the use of satire in the novel as the main contention of this paper. This content analysis focused on the thematic interpretation through the aesthetics of satire, humor, sarcasm, ridicule, hyperbole, and similar literary conceits to point out the societal issues and problems in the novel. The researcher also considered reader-response criticism to discern the main trope, food, in Bobis' work. Some technical devices in defamiliarization such as magic realism and social realism were also used to decipher the objects of satire. Moreover, Freudian and Lacanian psychoanalyses were employed as interpretative tools in unveiling the characters' representation and name symbols.

RESULTS AND DISCUSSION

Published simultaneously in Australia and Manila in 2005, and in the United States in 2009, Bobis' *Banana Heart Summer* is a novel about food and love. Divided into three parts-- "The Heart of the Matter"; "The Spleen of the Matter"; and "Becoming a Heart", the novel traces Nenita's coming of age in 50 chapters, each a discourse on local cuisine. Nenita's (or Nining's) experiences with food (both the cooking and the eating) are woven together with the love stories of the folk on Remedios Street. The novel offers awareness of the different types of poverty and issues brought along by the socio-historical and political problems where acceptance and forgiveness still prevail.

Overview of the Novel

Set in the summer of 1960s, the novel has Nenita as its main character. Based on the story, Nenita's eyes widen at the sight of Nana Dora's deep-fried caramelized bananas; her behavior seems like that of just another 12-year-old girl. Nenita believes in the myth of banana heart which she believed could to appease the hunger of her family as told by Nana Dora herself. Being the eldest, she tries to compensate for her father's being jobless but she gets her mother's rage in return. Maring beats Nenita even for a simple mistake which Nining considers as a sign of her *lihi* as she is conceiving her seventh child.

As the story progresses, Nenita witnesses the latest wares of the Calcium Man, the latest duet between the local Patsy Cline (Miss VV) and Roy Orbison (Mang Gusting), Manolito Ching's perfect hair, her father's stolen tongue and finally, her mother's latest lecture on dignity and the whims of her other five younger siblings.

As the summer days heat up, Nenita's simple pleasures of her childhood peel away, revealing the complex hearts of adults. She moves out of the tiny attic filled with seven other sleeping bodies to begin working as a maid for the Valenzuela family. Though living only next door, Nenita's new role as the breadwinner changes the family dynamic. Though immersed in her work, Nenita continues to witness such events in the neighborhood, including Miss VV's pregnancy with a married man, Mang Gusting's infidelity, the suicide of Tio Anding after Mr. Ching terminates him from his job, Manolito's guavas peeking from his shorts, the mayor's corruption during the eruption of the volcano, Gable Junior's first taste of imported corned beef where he got his welts, and the burial of their stillborn baby sister, Marinella.

Ralph Mckenna, the American friend of Ms. VV's father, Dr. Valenzuela, offers to marry Miss VV. They take Nining to America where she grows up and learns that there is no secret ingredient to obtaining acceptance, affection or answers—she can only try to forgive.

The tropes in the novel

As part of her aesthetics, Bobis uses trope in this novel. Trope or figurative thought is defined in The Columbia Dictionary of Modern Literary and Cultural Criticism as the usage that diverges from the norm. As one of the tropes used in the novel, food takes the role of expressing norms of the characters and the community as a whole. According to Mojares (2002), a complex story can be told from the meals in Philippine history. Citing Fernandez (1993) saying that cooking does not happen in midair or by whim, Mojares asserts that this story exists in real time and place, since it is shaped by real persons and occasions. Hence, Bobis' novel about food carries signification of cultural tradition represented by every meal.

Food is ever-present throughout *Banana Heart Summer* as it plays an important cultural and psychological role in the story. Hunger is central to Nenita's world and being. Food is used as a subject-matter set against the background of love as a human emotion. Love and food—associated with "hunger"—are two sides of the same coin. The novel explores what hunger is in the social context. Accordingly, Hefner describes hunger as that which we all experience. In addition, he describes it as "the greatest leveler of humankind, if it wishes to be leveled. But how and whether we appease it always restores the social order".

Each of the stories begins sweetly only to be edged with bitterness towards the end of the novel. The transitions in these stories should not be viewed entirely without sorrow; instead, they must be seen as an inevitable growth as characters begin to approach understanding of their lives. For Nenita, everything has a flavor and every flavor has its purpose. Bitterness holds as much importance as itscounterpart. However, it is in the mixing of the two that our deepest longings are confronted. To quote the narrator:

> -because hunger is always unsightly. It's our gut hanging out, unkempt like unassuaged love. We see it in someone else and instinctively we grab at our stomachs, then quickly withdraw our hands, knowing we have betrayed ourselves (p.187).

One of the characters, Nana Dora, is described similar to the jackfruit, which is "too prickly outside but sweet inside, but only if she was ripe enough to entertain your intrusions" (p.9) The preparation of the shredded heart in coconut milk is also aptly described:

> It must be the right heart, it must be the soft core of the right heart, it must be the yellowish part of the soft core of the right heart (p.10).

Nenita also has assumptions that the devil ate her father's tongue by cooking it in mushroom sauce, a similar method Spaniards follow in cooking ox tongue. The idea comes into her thoughts after her mother beats her, and her father keepshis silence as he always does, more likely after he lost his job. The "devil" refersto Gable's employer who terminates his job after finding cheaper labor for theextension of his house.

The *palitaw,* or the floated one, carries a similar impression with those whoeat it, such as the floating faith of Tiya Coring, the mother of Basilio Profundo. In the text, *palitaw* is likened to faith, as seen in the following excerpt:

> faith always floats, keeps us afloat. As it is in swimming, so it is in cooking, soit is in falling in love. We always believe we'll rise to the surface. Faith is too light to stay down, and it smells. We can't hide it (p. 20).

Further, this part of the novel describes that floating faith makes us brave and endure consequences. Dignity is also explained as may be lean but more filling than faith.

In the seventh and eighth chapters, Seaweed Salad" and the "Calcium Man with Pili nut husk on the Side" and the chapter titled, "Halo-halo: Mix-mixed Intentions" foretell the ideas on dignity and pride. The narrator recounts, "Mother said pride is a sin, but dignity is a savior".

The smoky coconut chicken in green papayas is used to present the strangeness behind an attempt to make the smell, taste, texture, or look of nature 'better'. In addition, the narrator states that the heart of the matter offends the palate, and when it does not offend, it scares. Thus, the text concludes, *"So we arm ourselves with herbs and spices, and we consider ourselves improved as a species"* (p. 49). This is similar to how each person lives and pretends as somebody else or has made-up identity.

The art of preserving is likened to the preparation and preservation of the taste of *acharra*, or preserved shredded and soaked green papayas in vinegar. For example, Maria Corazon Alano is described based on the speculations of the narrator as having an experiment of her new version of preserving domestic harmony. The text reads:

> *When in her heart, a wife decides that she's no longer one, not by her husband's decree or imputation, then she becomes playful. Without leaving, she can be single again, a maiden, a girl. The sense of old self can be recovered and preserved, where it had been adultered or diminished (p. 218).*

The strange synthesis of cookery, tales, and of human interaction is the dominant metaphorical theme of the novel, which, categorically speaking, appeals more to the intellect rather than to the senses. This appeal can be discerned amid the strewn metaphors that frequently appear in the novel.

The novel also attempts to establish a literary continuity between food preparation, consumption, and human relations and to present the facets of human relationships that can be explained creatively and understood in termsof food.

Analysis of the Banana Heart Summer

1. Characters
The characters in the first novel are semi-pathetic individuals seeking andaiming for hope, love, and acceptance. The narrator, both the 12-year-old Nining and the forty-year-old Nenita, longs for maternal love and acceptance, and after 29 years of working abroad, she longs for her country and hometown. Her mother, Marina and father Gable are also trying hard to find their proper places and responsibility for their children. Her mother's dignity is shattered by her inability to feed her family that may have caused her violent rage towards Nenita.Gable, is said to have his tongue eaten by the devil, hence his silence on whateveroccurs in the house.

Another character, Nana Dora, the cook, relies on some myths to sustain her hope of having her husband Tasyo back. Her husband left her because she failed to give him a child. After many years he follows Nana Dora, he sells seafoods which he peddles as "calcium, vitamins", possibly to seek for another chance thathe has never had.

Violeta Valenzuela or Miss VV, Nining's mistress is the most beautiful among the ladies on Remedios Street. She falls in love and gets pregnant by a marriedman. She eventually marries the man (Ralph Mckenna) who offers to save the grace of "Concepcion Immaculada".

Ralph Mckenna is an American who is old enough to be Ms. VV's father.Another character, Basilio Profundo, the bachelor who offers his love, throughhis mother's "floating faith" or *palitaw*, to Miss

VV but never wins her heart. Basilio is outsmarted by Mang Gusting, a married man, who is helplessly trapped in a marriage with Tiya Asun, who finds liberty in the delicacies that she prepares, making twists in the recipes and ingredients but with a deeper purpose of wanting to keep her marriage alive.

Moreover, through the narrator's encounter with Manolito Ching described as the Spanish-Chinese mestizo and the heir to the fortunes of the richest businessman in town, Nenita confirms the bitter reality of being poor. She narrates, "The poorest are whipped by the poor, and the poor are whipped by the rich, even without them lifting a finger" (p.31). Though the richest in the town, Manolito seems unhappy having busy parents, Mr. Ching and Señora Ching, who are respectively busy with getting richer and with personal effects like jewelry and dresses. The family of Mang Anding is considered the poorest in their street. After losing his job during a volcanic eruption, his wife being ill while his twins have nothing to eat, he commits suicide. Through his act, the reader views Mang Anding's helplessness as being very evident in his character; his family eventually receives help and full generosity of the neighbors during his wake and funeral.

Juanito Guapito, the 18-year-old son of Tiya Miling, elopes with Tiya Viring.. The two women are both storeowners who find rivalry not only in their stores but also in Juanito's heart. Tiya Viring is a "frozen delight" or spinster old enough to be her lover's mother and would be ready to be with someone just "not to miss the last trip". When they elope, they go to the fringe garden of Boy Hapon, who is rarely seen in the neighborhood thus the speculations of coming from nowhere and the one who invoked the volcanos' eruption. Later in the novel, Nining learns that Boy Hapon is an ordinary person just like her, the twins Chichi and Bebet and the other folks in the neighborhood and inside his hut is collection of romance pocketbooks. Boy Hapon also tells her that his mother worked for the Japanese which explains his looks; that is also the reason why others don't like him there.

Critically speaking, one can say that every character, in general, aims for his or her particular desires. The novel presents each of them as being unsatisfied with what he or she has. The characters expect for something. Borrowing Freud's concepts, Lacan declares that the unconscious is structured like a language; therefore linguistics and semiotics may be used to study it.

2. Structure and Style

In this paper, structure refers to the presentation of the story. It is the manner by which the author presents the chronology of events. Style, according to Abrams (1999: 303) "is the manner of linguistic expression in prose or verse- as how speakers or writers say whatever it is that they say."

The story is told in the first-person point of view by a 40-year-old migrant worker named Nenita. Her tale traces her life's events when she was only 12 years old, in her hometown, longing for the love of her mother. The 12-year-old Nenita, based on the 40-year-old narrator's tales, aims to be of worth to her family particularly to her mother by being a good cook and literally a food provider. It was when she heard of the myth of the banana heart and decided to get hold of it.

Nenita enumerates her townsfolk and describes each character while revealing how these characters are interrelated. In so doing, she vividly describes every dish representing each character and the manner of preparing it.

Nenita's description of each character is full of innocence of a child (e.g. how she narrates that babies come out from armpits after hearing her parents gasping for air from the vent). Such can be discerned from the following excerpts:

> -to hold her tightly at night, whispering over and over again, I love you Maring, I love you. Then a baby always arrived from the armpit (p.71)

-which clung to the waist of our father who clung to our mother and whispered, I love you, I love you, while she kept her face turned away, breathing precious air from the vent (p. 73-74)

After narrating an event, the narrator fast-forwards to present events such as when she recounts the evening when her brother suddenly got hungry after listening to the "predictable breathing" that came from the other side of the mat. Specifically, Nenita shifts to this:

This was a story that he would tell me years later in his weary letters, which always asked whether I could send the family's a little bit of help (p. 202.)

The narrator also talks about falling in love at a very young age. She describes her ability and inability to understand things as a child. When Manolito volunteers to climb the guava tree, Nining and Chichi see his "two guavas" peeking out from his shorts.

Two guavas, two guavas, she said swallowing a fresh burst of giggles. I looked up. My cheeks were on fire. Was it a fruit of a vegetable? Up there, Manolito Chong's shorts were too shorts indeed. (p. 122)

But how can I save that twelve-year-old from these arguments? Of course I love my own? Even today, it takes great effort to believe myself (p.131).

I could climb any tree at my time (p. 132).

The narrative also reveals the child's lack of ability to understand the difference between 'stolen and the bought taste'.

That summer I was twelve, lihi made sense. Mother vented her spleen on me because she was pregnant, and she couldn't help it. Today, twenty years later, and so far away from home, I understand and I forgive (p. 103).

3. Theme

In the book, material poverty coexists alongside spiritual poverty. The former functions as a dual role that fuels Nenita's endless pursuit of maternal love. The novel depicts an aching need for acceptance and love in the lives of those who live on Remedios Street during that summer. The dramas of other characters' relationship and love help the narrator as she struggles to satisfy her need to establish a relationship with her abusive mother. Undeniably, most characters are individuals who are eternally searching for inner peace.

The nourishment of body and soul is the most sought-after idea in the novel as the narrator and other characters long for satisfaction and fulfilment of their desires. For example, Nenita's longing for her mother Maring's maternal love is Nenita's motivation to seek for a local and eventually foreign employment at a young age. Maring's yearning for the acceptance of her parents and society for marrying a mason is seen through her personal idea of dignity and pride. Miss VV's decision to marry a man old enough to be her father could represent a refuge for the love that she can never have. Nana Dora's beliefs in myths could be attributed to her desires such as her husband's coming home.

4. Tone

Tone or intonation refers to the expression of a literary speaker towards his reader or listener. Abrams discusses tone further in the following statements:

> *The tone of a speech can be described as critical or approving, formal or intimate, outspoken or reticent, solemn or playful, arrogant or prayerful, angry or loving, serious or ironic, condescending or obsequious, and so on through numberless possible nuances of relationship and attitude both to object and auditor. (Abrams:1999: 218)*

The entire novel is literarily written even with its obvious attempt to break conventions in writing given Bobis" inclination to touches of satire. The satires are evident in the use of various metaphors throughout the narrative; these metaphors sounds loving but have serious meaning that requires readers to understand the undertones more deeply. The author also resorts to writing on serious subjects in lighter tone making the readers feel light rather than bored or scared. The nostalgic pattern of the narrator's recounting her experiences reflects her actual childhood involvements in the neighborhood that have led to her coming of age and full understanding of her life and those of others. Note in these lines, where the narrator talks about how Nining's siblings quarrel over pork knuckles, Nining's innocence reveals a certain reality with her mistress:

Claro began to cry. Nilo chanted, "greedy, greedy!" The two youngest joined in, banging their hands on the table.

"Stop acting like pigs! Mother screamed.

Junior giggled. 'No, we're not- this is pig, he said under his breath, then bit the flesh hanging from the knuckle. (229-230)

You see, right after her loss, Tiya Miling began speaking in tongues, inventing fresh terminology for 'that evil woman who stole my son". I must admit I was confused when I overheard something about teeth, as they shuffled cards. "Please, what's "a woman with loose molars"? I asked my mistress.

Violeta Valenzuela could not answer. Her face was torn between laughter and guilt, neither of which I understood. Loose morals. She could not enlighten me about my confused consonants. She searched my face for any sign of accusation. (p.145)

The excerpts above simply disclose social problems like poverty, gambling, gossiping and morality issues. Hunger may cause people to be greedy and at the same disrespectful. The issue of talking about others behind their back while playing cards is inherent in the barrio folks. Thus, when Nining innocently asks for the meaning of "woman with loose molars", her mistress feels guilty of being one.

The aesthetics of satire in the novel
What is satire?

Satire is a form of literature, which, according to Hornedo, is just like ode, lyric, panegyric, elegy, lampoon, caricature, comedy, tragedy, and romance. A satire primarily seeks to ridicule or criticize any subject, idea, institution ormankind in general. However, the satirist also seeks to expose some representative vices that are considered threat or harmful in the society. In addition, a satire aimsto point out human behavior that is despicable and hence, needs to be changed. The goal of a satire can be either destruction or reform but mainly for the generalbenefit or betterment of humanity as a whole.

In general, there are two identified satirical styles—direct and indirect. Adirect satire is that which is directly stated; an indirect one is communicated or implied through characters in a situation. The two well-known types of satire are the Horatian, described as intended for fun which is light-hearted, and the Juvenalian, the bitter, attacking and angry in nature. Beckson and Ganz (1960) explain that the treatment and attitude rather than the subject matter mark thepresence of satire.

Satirical techniques and devices

There is a variety of satirical techniques and devices which can be used tocomment on or criticize a particular subject or character. Some of them are irony,hyperbole, paradox, palindrome, oxymoron, magic realism and social realism. Inaddition to these, defamiliarization is also a technical satirical device like tropes and conceits.

As a technique, defamiliarization uses devices like tropes, metaphors, magic realism, and social realism to present ideas in an unfamiliar artistic form purposively to stimulate fresh perception. Viktor Shklovsky (1993), one of themain voices behind a way of thinking about literature which is known today asRussian Formalism, is concerned more with the notion of *literariness*. Accordingto him, literariness is the result of working language so that it "makes strange" orinterrupts our habituated or automatic perception of the word. By interruptingour automatic perception of the word in this way, the reader is forced to makeextra effort to determine the meaning of the text and in so doing, the reader'swonder of the world is re-enlivened. Hence, *defamiliarization* can be defined as the technique by which the author seeks to re-enliven the naturally inquisitive and literally awesome gaze of the child in the reader. As applied in literature, defamiliarization works in three levels: language, content, and literary forms. Needless to say, the entire novel applies these three levels.

With regard to the novel's tone, the narrative is evidently told in a way that thereader will become apathetic towards the characters, except towards the narrator who innocently tells of her experiences as a child. The following are the various satirical tropes readers can identify in the novel. For clarity, they are presentedaccording to type:

1. Exaggeration

Exaggeration aims to represent something beyond the ordinary and make it appear ridiculous so that the readers can identify the subjected flaws of the individual or society as a whole. Under exaggeration are caricature and burlesque. The former exaggerates physical features or traits while the latter deals with the exaggeration of style through language or action. Hyperbole and farce may also be classified under this type since both utilize exaggeration through language andsituations.

To illustrate exaggeration, here are a few excerpts from the novel, in which thenarrator describes Tiyo Anding and Tiya Asun's family as the poorest in the street. The narrator also compares their family's nothingness to theirs:

I wondered what they ate; their house hardly smelled of cooking. We had been eating more –water-than-rice gruel for a week after my father's and, of course, her husband's sacking. I wondered what non-smelling thing boiled in Tiya Asun's pots. In my heart I knew that her family felt it too- the esophagus lengthening, I mean. And as they were poorer than us, perhaps other parts inevitably followed

*suit- the tongue, the cheeks, and the eyes, perhaps stretching towards
the earth, as if they were already being pulled into their graves. (26)*

The excerpts above suggest that the narrator compares hunger to how
poverty reeks in their street. The description of Tiya Asun, having
no breasts, no hips, no brows and little hair added to the exaggerated
faces of scarcity in all levels— material and physical.

Another form of exaggeration is shown in the character of Señora
Ching. She is a full–blooded Spaniard who wears mantilla, a lace or silk
veil or shawl worn over the head and shoulders, often over a high
comb called a peineta, popular with women in Spain. The narrator
describes Senora Ching in the following lines when she catches the
narrator holding a bottle of an *ube* jam in their kitchen.

*She wore an emerald silk robe with red dragons—she had a
penchant for fire- breathing things—and the most beautiful
tortoiseshell comb with gold studs, angled gracefully on the side
of her low chignon. (38)*

A full-blooded Spaniard, married with a Chinese creates a disaster in
the line of fashion. This form of satirical caricature is somewhat similar to
Rizal's Doña Victorina. Likewise, her act of screaming because she sees
a thief in the 12-year-old girl holding a bottle of jam inside her own
kitchen is indeed an exaggeration.

2. Incongruity

Incongruity is used to present things or ideas that are absurd or out of
place. Included in this second group are irony, oxymoron, metaphor,
and paradox. The actual intent of irony is to express the opposite
meaning of words. There are four types of irony; verbal, which is
simply an inversion of meaning; dramatic, when the words or actions
carry another meaning in contrast between the speaker/ character
and its audience/reader; socratic, or feigning or pretending ignorance
to achieve its intended effect over an opponent; and situational, the
type which is dependent on the inconsistency between purpose and

results. Both oxymoron and paradox use contradiction of something through language and action to present the real idea or situation.

One example of ironic circumstance in the novel is shown during the volcanic eruption, which the residents of Remedios Street found ordinary, and being so, it will not stop the celebration of their fiesta. That foreign aid will abound and will be the subject of politician's corruption is a known fact, and so applied in the novel, local canned goods shall be labelled with their names and the imported ones will go to the black market to allow the industry of the already rich businessmen to flourish. By businessmen, the novel refers to those who are closely related to the mayor. The "one eruption, one mansion" is said to be the likely epitaph on the mayor's tomb when he dies. The time of calamity turns out as a prosperous time for the residents and the greedy politicians. The locals are able to taste foreign products from the black market, so little do they know that those goods were supposed to be given to them for free.

The generosity of the neighborhood when Mang Anding commits suicide is another example of incongruity. The novel implies that his family is the poorest yet nobody offers help. It is during his wake and funeral when everybody becomes 'helpful". The Chings family give five hundred pesos, for the funeral services. Whatever help the family received during the wake and funeral will never bring back Mang Anding's life; ironically, their help will bury him instead.

3. Parody

The third group, parody, is used to ridicule the original through imitation of a usually serious piece of work. Travesty falls under this group; it presents a usually religious subject playfully reducing it to the lowest level of mockery.

Chapter 42 of the novel is entitled *Cosido: soup of immaculada concepcion.* A sour soup, cocido is what one sees in front of Mang Gusting Alano and Miss VV while they discuss about the unwanted pregnancy that results from their illicit affair. In their conversation, the characters use "folk aphorisms" so that Nining will not understand the subject of their conversation. Note how the narrator uses Biblical characters' names to refer to themselves. Note in the following lines:

But we can't- you can't have that- that Concepcion Immaculada, even if- ifSaint Joseph loves Mary.(213)

Saint Joseph will always love Mary- but I'm sorry, I can't..(214)

I wish Saint Joseph were dead. (215)

Indeed, the holy figure of Mama Mary, who conceived without sin, is used to relate to Miss VV's unwanted pregnancy. The statement also suggests a blasphemy as one of the characters wishes for the death of a Saint Joseph, referring to the married man's inability to leave his wife and give his name to the unborn child.

The same is true in the following line:

I only want to cook good, I only want to eat good, I only want to be good. (14)

The above line shows the words that Nining tells to herself as her own novena instead of actual Catholic prayer in her intention to help and put food onto the family's table. The novena is mentioned in the novel as a repetitive prayer, which Nining recites while being beaten by her mother.

4. Reversal

Reversal focuses on the use of order of things or ideas such as a hierarchical order or events. Palindrome, the use of a word, phrase or number that reads the same backward or forward can be identified under this fourth group.

The reversal in the novel is evident in the character of Nining. She is just 12 years old, yet she already wants to help feed the family. Her first earning amounting to four pesos is even higher than the last wage her father brought home after he had lost his job. Nenita can think better and decide more sensibly than his father whose tongue was "eaten by the devil" according to the narrative. When Nining innocently asks for the meaning of "woman with loose molars", her mistress felt guilty of being one, "a woman with loose morals". The position of the two letters in both words creates confusion between the words themselves, yet the paranoia is obvious to a person who knows better but has failed to act accordingly.

CONCLUSIONS

The novel boasts of numerous satirical tropes intended to ridicule the follies and foibles of society. The idea of child labor and child abuse is just one of the issues in the reality frame which the novel discloses. At 12 years old, Nining is forced to stop attending school and volunteers to help the family by working as a maid. In return, she receives her mother's rage with slaps and blows that hurt her, and one time even burns her skin. Afterwards, she feeds her. This instance is accepted by Nining as part of her mother's *lihi* which later on she understands as a defense mechanism disguised as dignity. The problems of illicit affair, corruption, and rampant moral degradation made through gossips among the neighborhood are just some of the issues unraveled in the novel using metaphorical representations of food.

Bobis' intentional use of defamiliarization opens the reader to the possibility of understanding the culture of the community represented by the novel's setting. The aesthetics of satire intends to create realization on the reader's point of view to appreciate the work of fiction and at the same time to be mindful of the biting realities of life. The entire novel is full of lines that reveal thoughtful concerns presented in a way that the reader shall find amusing yet needs to be changed. The Bicolanos are Filipinos whose ideas and ideals may emanate from their inherent desires and their promulgation rooted from the type of culture that they have. Just as Rizal's novels satirize the Filipino's characters and attitudes against Spaniards, Bobis' novel also aims to call for a change and positivity amidst the cultural idiocies of the Filipinos particularly Bicolanos.

The researcher, therefore, recommends that creative writing be treated with purpose. Literature is not just for entertainment; more so, it is supposed to suggest, inform, and educate, and must serve their worth if taught well in institutions. Literature should not just instill critical thinking in the readers butalso stir their emotions to respond to the call for change as Bobis' work highlyencourages.

TRANSLATIONAL RESEARCH

With the technological advancement in today's society, the current trend demands the function, access and application of literature through the worldwide web or commonly called "Internet". The present generation called "digital natives" can easily manipulate and grasp ideas from the available internet sources.

Most of these digital natives easily get bored with books, and seldom devote time in reading. Through various representation of ideas employing technology, information may instill attraction to the learners. This paper also recommends the use of popular culture specifically satirical comic strips similar to the Japanesemanga. Manga in Japanese means "flowing words" or "Undisciplined words",an ancient art that has been used as a form of entertainment (Simon, 2003). The satirical comic strips may be an example of an innovative media that can be accessible not only in the Philippines but also in the global community.

LITERATURE CITED

Abrams, M.H. (1953). *The mirror and the lamp:* Romantic theory and the critical tradition. Oxford: Oxford University Press Inc.

Abrams M.H. (1999). A glossary of literary terms: Seventh edition. Cornell. Cornell University.

Bobis, M. (2005). Banana heart summer. Pasig City, Philippines: Anvil

Publishing Inc..

Clifford, G. (1973). The interpretation of cultures. New York: Basic, 412 453.

Colayco, C. (1957). The Novelist: A portrait painter. UNITAS, 30 (4), 840-848.Santos, P.V.M (2003). Hagkus: Twentieth century Bikol women writers: De La Salle University Press, Inc.

Fernandez, D. (1988). Culture ingested: Notes on the indigenization of food. Philippine Studies, 36 (2), 219-232

Hornedo F.H. (2001). Ideas and ideals: Essays in Filipino cognitive history. Manila, Philippines: UST Publishing house.

Hornedo, F.H.(2002). Pagpapakatao and other essays in Contemporary Philosophy and Literature of Ideas. Manila, Philippines: UST Publishing House.

Lumbera, B. (1997). Revaluation 1997: Essays on Philippine literature, cinema & popular culture. Manila, Philippines: UST Publishing House.

Makaryk, I.R.ed. (1993). Encyclopedia of contemporary literary theory: Approaches, scholars, terms. Canada, University of Toronto press Inc.

Simon, B. (2003). Manga. Urban Dictionary. Retrieved from http://www. urbandictionary.com/define.php?term=manga retrieved on April 11, 2015.

Sy-Ng, MCB. (2011). The heart of the matter: A Lacanian unveiling of the unconscious discourse in Banana Heart Summer. Ad Veritatem, 1 (1), 239- 257.

Sy MB.(2013). Humor in Alejandro Roces' Fiction. IAMURE International Journal of Literature, Philosophy and Religion. 4, (June), 85-98

Tian, X. (2014) Uncertain Satire in Modern Chinese Fiction and Drama: 1930-1949 Retrieved from http://escholarship.org./uc/item/1g94d1hb

The Asia Foundation (2015). The Asia Foundation's Jaime Faustino Participates in USAID-UNCDF Extreme Poverty Conference.

Retrieved from http:// asiafoundation.org/news/2015/04/the-asia-foundations-jaime-faustino-   participates-in-usaid-uncdf-extreme-poverty-conference/

4

Star for a Cause: A Lacanian Review of *The SolemnLantern Maker*

Published in United International Journal for Research & Technology
Volume 02, Issue 03, 2021 | ISSN: 2582-6832

ABSTRACT

This paper aims to present Lacanian analysis of the novel, The Solemn Lantern Maker of Merlinda Bobis, a Filipino transnational writer. The formalistic approach was employed in the literary analysis of the elements of fiction, contextual representation of star as the novel's trope, and the societal problems depicted in the novel. It aims to introduce a paper that may be usedin a teaching-learning scenario that evaluates and criticizes, anchored on the philosophical theory of Lacan on psychoanalysis. Saussere's linguistic as used in Lacan's psychoanalysis, traced the formalistic analysis in terms of characters and the trope, referring to the contextualization and symbolic meaning of star. The setting, structure and style, language and local color are suggestive of the foregrounding of the unconscious. The novel can be concluded as an expression of the author's speculation of the mechanism whereby an individual emerges into consciousness. The entire novel is suggestive of action that should emanate from the self, towards helping the community by being aware of the societal follies and angst originated from the colonial mentality brought by the country's course of history. It is recommended that the learning materials with realistic portrayal be treated with appropriate analytical tool.

Keywords: Lacanian analysis, psychoanalysis, Solemn Lantern Maker, Merlinda Bobis, Philippines.

INTRODUCTION

The Solemn Lantern Maker is a novel about star and silence published in Australia in 2008 and the following year in United States of America. It has 112 episodes/chapters divided into six days before Christmas, December 19 to December 24. The main character, ten-year old Noland is a mute, due to traumatic experience. The novel portrays binary oppositions such as powerless and powerful, Third-world country poverty and white- Western affluence with the balance on global and local issues. It talks about poverty, child prostitution, land struggles, and political corruption. They are the evident societal issues in the Philippines. The characters, amidst exploitations, bad memories and silences, exhibit hope for the better future. The novel's author, Bobis resides and works in Wollongong, Australia, but hailed from the province of Albay in the Bicol region, southern part of the Philippines. She is an expatriate writer, a Filipino author who stays in another country but most of her works' subject is her own country. She writes in three tongues and in different genre where she proves her excellence in all her works through various awards and recognition. In general, she sees her country's need for liberation and search for cultural strength. Her being transnational motivates her to write from her perspective of Philippine culture associated with her personal experiences in other country. She wants her readers to understand her works from the recognition of society behind the creative representation of political and cultural flaws.

Objectives

This paper aims to introduce a reading material that may be used in a teaching-learning scenario which is based on the evaluation and analysis anchored on the philosophical theory of Lacan on psychoanalysis. Specifically, this paper deals on the formalistic evaluation of the elements of fiction focused on the characters' journey to self-fortification to reveal the socio-political and cultural angsts and the hegemony of power. Alongside, this paper also aims to disclose the contextual representation of stars behind the use of tropes in the narrative. Moreover, this paper also traces the cultural background of the Philippine underneath its tint of colonial mentality. This paper poses a reading material that serves not just a mere form of entertainment but also on discovering the reader's critical ability which is Lacan's idea on discovering oneself.

METHODOLOGY

The analysis of The Solemn Lantern Maker, Bobis' second novel is anchored on Lacan's concept of psychoanalysis which is applied in the understanding of the characters, their journey alongside their order of need, demand and desire. The formalistic evaluation of the novel including the setting, structure and style, tone, theme and the discussions of the societal issues led to the unveiling of the unconscious to conscious pattern as the reflection of the intrinsic complexities of the psyche. The trope was also used to reveal the hegemony of power and the hidden colonial mentality behind the contextual representation of star in various instances.

Theoretical Framework

The Lacanian framework as applied in this paper claimsthat even if the signifiers are visual, they are treated as if they were verbal. Accordingly, "signifiers may only be interpreted when placed in a verbal context through chains of association" (Grosz, 2001,p 92-114). Thispaper used Lacan's studies on the psychoanalysis and linguistics as theoretical framework, to show primarily how the conscious discourse veils the unconscious meaning.

Jaques Lacan (1901-1981) was a French psychoanalyst who re conceptualized Freud using post-structuralism. He sought to return psychoanalysis on the unconscious, using Saussure's linguistics, structural anthropology and post-structural theories. Lacan's foregrounding of the unconscious lends to his speculation of the mechanism whereby an individual emerges into consciousness. Before the sense of self emerges, the young child existsin a realm, which Lacan calls the imaginary (pre- Oedipal), in which there is no distinction between the self and the other and there is an idealized identificationwith the mother. The child experiences both itself and its environment as a random, fragmented and formless mass. This paper shall follow the discussion of the novelidentifying Lacan's three orders- the imaginary, thesymbolic and the real.

RESULTS AND DISCUSSION

1. *The main character's Journey to self-fortification:Noland and Nena's Silent Space, A Star studded silent but loud cry for help*

The main character, Noland is a lantern maker. He has been "silent" for four years. He is fascinated with angelsand stars which clippings and sketches he keeps in his notebook. He basically believes that a star has five lightsand angels live in stars.

This is how he is described at the beginning of the narrative:

Noland raises five fingers thrice to indicate fifteen pesos. Intent on his dinner, the man didnot see the price. "how much?' he asks again. Noland raises his palm close to the man's facerepeating the gesture. The man pauses, stares- The man pays with a fifty-peso bill. Noland shakes his head and shows an empty palm. Nochange. Sorry sir. Perhaps two more stars? Heoffers a green one this time and another red.

"No, keep the change". He waves the boy away and hangs the star on his window, just above the wheel. Thenas an afterthought, "You mute, kid?"

The ten-year old nods.(pp.4-5)

Noland helps his mother earn their living through the colorful lanterns that he sells with his friend. They are living in a "box" called hut in the intersection of the city. It is made up of scraps of corrugated iron, wood, cardboard and plastic. They have been living in the slums area for two years. Later in the narrative, Noland becomes a subject of interest of a Japanese who gave him hundred dollars, food, new clothes and shoes in exchange of his photos taken in the hotel room. It worsens his trauma when the police "rescued" the American woman from their hut. Noland and his motherwere brought to the precinct for detention and interrogation. In the epilogue, he is in a different house where he cannot see angels but remembers stars in the sky and hill.

Nena is Noland's mother, a laundry woman whose legs were crippled four years earlier, the same time when hisson acquires his "silence". She has a trauma with "uniforms" and protects his son to the most that she can. She opposes the idea of helping the American woman lest it might cause them trouble. In the course of the narrative, she still takes care of the woman, offers her herbal medicine, and considers that she did it for her son.

Noland's character is a victim of circumstances, of incidents around him. His only desire is to help "the angel" who fell from the sky. He only wants to decorate their house with pictures of stars and angels. He only wants to prepare designs of his lanterns in a notebook and to keep a picture of his mother with a young boy. Yet, it turns out that his simple wishes can be interpreted as a grim ploy of a terrorist conspiracy. Nena, on the other hand, is an archetype of a protective mother whose basic intention is to provide support and look after her son. There is a part in the narrative which suggests that she somehow feels jealous with their "guest. Generally, mother and son are both victims of situations that are beyond their control.

The above discussion on the mother and son showed an account of the mirror stage which is Lacan's most famous theoretical contribution. For Lacan, the Freudian Oedipus complex stages the drama of the child's laborious struggles to situate him/her-self vis-à-vis all three register-theoretic dimensions of Otherness. The child's identifications with maternal and paternal Others are distributed across Real and Symbolic dimensions.

However, different subjects-in-formation distribute their identifications differently.

1.1 Other Character's Symbolic Order of Need, Demand and Desire

The understanding of the other characters in the novel provides the readers to decipher the main intention of the author as declared that the unconscious is structured like a language. Hence, linguistics and semiotics may be used in the analysis. (Grosz, 87).

According to Lacan, one of the (if not the) most significant and indispensable conditions of possibility for singular subjectivity is the collective symbolic order. Individual subjects are what they are in and through the mediation of the socio-linguistic arrangements and constellations of the register of the Symbolic.

A. *Elvis and Bobby Cool*

Elvis is a street boy who helps Noland sells his wares. He also works as a prostitute in exchange of his basic needs, like money, food and clothes. He cares about Noland like his own brother. Aside from helping him sells the lanterns, he tours Noland around, gives him money as a "share" from his 'business profit" and treats him with food. When Noland becomes the target of the Japanese pedophile, he offers to do double work just to spare Noland from such "job".

After the hotel incident, Elvis fights back the pimp, who beats him in return and accuses him of having no sense of gratitude. He then tries to search for possible salvation when he visits the church and finding none, he continues with his known "business" even to locals whom he finds cheap. Elvis was shot by the police who are made to believe that he is the mastermind of the "terrorist attack" against the American woman.

Bobby Cool prides himself with the kind of job he offers to Elvis. He himself has been in the business and liberates himself after finding Elvis whom he considers as a "jackpot". He teaches Elvis the art of "becoming rich" through his language-English, the language of the customers and through wearing imitation of apparel brands. When Elvis fights him because of Noland, he loses his main source of income.

Elvis and Bobby are both victims of the pedophile industry in their own country. Such "industry" benefits the foreigners more because it is fueled by the cancer of poverty from the less fortunate children.

With poverty at hand, the main focus is survival and morality does not matter. The narrative did not provide a redeeming condition in their characters. Elvis got killed and Bobby might probably find another willing victim of his business.

B. Cate Burns

The American woman, Cate Burns arrives in the Philippines for a vacation, to unwind and rest her heart and mind from the disappointment towards her husband who does not want their child in her womb. She gets involved in the shooting of a journalist when she was "rescued" by Noland and Elvis who considers her an "angel". Her identity was only revealed through the news in the television. She temporarily suffered from amnesia due to trauma caused by the shooting and her miscarriage. When she was "rescued" from the hut and brought to the hospital, she wants to help the people who also helped her, but to no avail. The case of "missing American" was interpreted as a terrorist attack of the Abu Sayaff group.

Later in the narrative, everything becomes clearer as Cate remembers how it all started. She is a student in Cornell pursuing a doctorate degree in Literature and took off to another country without the knowledge of her husband. She recalls the incident before her flight to the Philippines from the taxi ride to the airport on the other side of the world "from a sleek apartment at leafy Cornell with a man in the bed whose smell is still on her. She has the imprint of his unwelcome lovemaking in the early hours" (p.220).

This is how she recounts the comparison between child and tax evasion:

> *Cook up the books for debit, cry poor, or poor me, and wait*
> *for the taxman to validate your withdrawal from the ranks*
> *of fatherhood. (p. 221)*

Cate Burns is a woman who longs for love and liberty. When she decided to leave her husband, it brings her to a different scenario where she lost her child, and temporarily her own identity. She also lost her chance to help the mother and child, whom she knows are the ones who need protection. In her mind, she knows she can help but being controlled by some forces, physical and political; she is helpless.

C. *Germinio De Vera and Lydia De Vera*

Germinio de Vera is the man who was shot by the PizzaHut man. He was a journalist famous for his daring exposés on corruption and extra-judicial killings.

This is how the narrative describes the news that reveals the motive of De Vera's murder.

> *The news speculates that Germinio De Vera was salvaged for exposing a senator's "friendship" with a famous Jueteng King, the godfather of illegal gambling. Perhaps the senator's election campaign was funded by this generous personage? But the journalist pushed his own luck further, throwing the deadly card on the table with the questions: Was the senator the Jueteng King himself? The answer was a speedy salvaging, on a motorcycle. (p. 59)*

Lydia de Vera is the widow of Germinio De Vera. She organizes a public campaign against her husband's murderer. She finds her husband's old files on every corrupt official in the country and his newspaper articles that grew bolder through the years. She realizes that the bravery of her husband is at the same time his stupidity.

The couple is called "the young activist couple, the "idealists", the "radical couple". It signifies their compatibility in profession, being a journalist and a political science graduate. Their principle turns them into victims of the system, Germinio, the allegedly hero is considered the enemy and a fool. Lydia de Vera lost her love, her Jimmy, the husband for only two years. She was not able to do anything even at the later part of the narrative although she has the old files of her late husband. It is a life, love, and principle wasted in the societal chaos.

D. Senator GB or Good Boy Buracher

The senator is the one accused of being friends with the godfather of illegal gambling. He is the one pursued by Germinio De Vera and after the murder, pursued by another reporter. This is how the reporter interrogates him:

> Senator, what about the fact that the deceased exposed your alleged involvement with illegal gambling, that you're possibly one of its big bosses, and that someone, in fact, overheard you threaten to "mow-down any two-bit journalist' who messes with your so-called 'operations'0 what do you say to that senator?

> And senator, do you think there's any connections between Germinio De Vera's murder and the kidnapping of cate Burns? (p. 146)

The senator earned his nickname "Good Boy" from his religious charities where his wife who is twenty years his junior sings after they got married. He is described in the narrative who likes indirect influences. As such,"he can speak to his friends who will make sure someone loses his job if this isn't handled his way" (p.217)

It can be gleaned from the way the senator reacts that he is guilty of the said accusations. When the TV news keeps showing the innocent face of the accused boy, he curses the TV and speaks his mind that, "if there's any more tugging at the heartstrings, they'll snap". It goes to show that his character wants to be freed from what he is actually guilty of. He will do anything at the expense of others, just to stay in his comfort zone, free from the accusations of which he is guilty of. He wants temporary peace, through forgetting his conscience when he is with his young wife and daughter.

E. Colonel David Lan

Colonel Lane is an American in charge of the "search and rescue operation" of the missing American, Cate Burns. He is called" people's colonel", being a model soldier from Afghanistan after the 9/11 attack in the US. He also tries to persuade the consul from the US embassy to help Cate Burns with her wish, about saving the mother and son. He had been warned to mind his business instead and it does not include saving other people who are not his people. He recounts the issue of Philippine-American relationship as presented in these excerpts from the narrative:

> David hears the equal bitterness of the Filipina journalist on the television panel. After a while, he whispers tiredly, "Forty years Bettina. We occupied them for forty years and before that, we fought them in a war, and much later, we backed the dictator who robbed them blind for twenty years (216).

His character serves as an example of a willing victim of forces around him. He has a duty to fulfill yet not being able to do it at his own will and decision. His frustration left him restless that he can be likened to a prisoner. A captive of his duty as a soldier and husband, a person torn between his domestic life and country's call.

F. Colonel Roberto Espinosa

Roberto Espinosa is the chief of Special Projects. Special Projects include the Philippine government programs to combat against forces that serve as threat to its people. One of it is the Balikatan or the shoulder to shoulder fight with the US against possible attack of terrorism. Espinosa was able to "bag" the evidences found in the hut such as the stars, the notebook, the dollar, and the clippings. He also disguises as an ally of Nena and Noland who are the victims turned culprits of a controversial murder. This is how his thoughts are described in the narrative:

> *Ah, there's blood on all our hands. He studies the photos of the boys again, trapped in a star. Yes, save the senator and save himself, his job, save everyone. A safe house then, safe from the news cannibals until the New Year, and maybe, just maybe- he mulls over possibilities, over the faces on the star. It must be the angels for where can this inspiration springs from? He wants to save one boy, at least the one he knows, but the older one makes him drop his eyes. (p. 239)*

Later, his character knew full well that the mother and son are innocent. The 'truth' from the notebook, which others consider as the "terrorist- attack evidence" landed on his desk.

He receives phone calls that stir his sense of judgment and make him contemplate on what to do. Finally, like the other characters in the narrative, he was destined to be a captive of the system. It is the sense of survival that still succeeded. In a system run by people in power, there is an extensive manipulation of truth.

G. *Eugene Costa*

Described as the stalker young journalist, Eugene Costa pursues the case of the murder and the missing American. He tries to interview the senator only to be moved aside by his bodyguards. He believes in the same idea that Germinio De Vera was murdered because of his exposés.

His character is another archetype of a dutiful person, tied to the obligation of his work. He is physically and emotionally tired and longing for sleep and vacation in the province. Yet, he is mandated to seek the truth, despite his fright from being aware that anyone telling the truth can be murdered.

H. *Mario and Helen, Mang Pedring and Manang Betya*

Mario and Helen are a couple who has no offspring. Their source of income is the pirated video films they play in their hut in the intersection. Mario is fond of cockfight while Helen gossips and befriends their neighbors to catch fresh stories for the day. When she saw Cate Burns in front of their neighbors' hut, she manages to inform the authorities with the thought that she will get a reward.

Mang Pedring is called the "wire-man" in the intersection who provides illegal connection of electricity through his bag of tools in exchange of a certain fee. Manang Betya is also one of their neighbors. She always holds a rosary in one hand and the other holds the notebook she uses for jueteng, an illegal gambling racket.

They are characters who are examples of common people who face daily struggles of survival. They mirror the kind of Filipinos who are fond of vices like gossiping and different types of gambling. They relied their source of living from business done in an illegal way. At the later part of the narrative, they all sought self-fortification against the "crime" done by their neighbors, trying to justify that they are better than them.

I. *Mang Gusting, Mikmik, and Lisa*

Mang Gusting is the store owner in the intersection. He has a karaoke that adds to the life of the nightly drinking spree. His wife left for Hongkong as an OFW and never came back. He is unaware of her charges there while he seeks for the satisfaction of his biological needs through Liza. She is one of the "karaoke women" at night and the washerwomen during the day. Nena lost the only client of her laundry over her. Michaela or Mikmik is the daughter of Mang Gusting. Like any other child who longs for a mother and grows up with only a father, she seeks companionship with her "gang" and learns that things can be acquired through pretension.

Those three characters are also representatives of people with their own desires. They cope with their longing through any available immediate means that they could have. Each takes an opportunistic way of getting through with the society at the expense of others.

2. *Setting*

The novel is set in the Philippines, in the heart of the city of Manila, its capital. The narrative expresses its history through the description of places that the characters explore. Primarily, Chapter 1 has description provided in the thought of the narrator, *palm as small as star, star as small as a country. My country's children, small as hope. (pp. 4-5)*

> One of the characters explicitly introduces the place to the American woman this way: *Nena is excited. Philippines, you know, good, good. Philippines here, Manila here, my house here, you here, okay (p. 88).*

The narrative provides a photographic image of the slums, where corrugated iron, cardboards, and plastic make up a shelter or houses. The communities of the rich and the poor are both described through the representation of their ways of living. The senator's lavish living is presented by the mention of some appliances like his own home theater.

Likewise, the area like Quiapo where the "religiousvendors" of herbs used to abort a fetus, abound, along with the folks with so much catholic faith and worship the black Nazarene, is also described. Other landmarks are described such as Plaza Miranda where political bombing happened in 1972 during the dictator's years ofmartial law; the Star City, "where Noland can find all the rides of his dreams"; CCP the Cultural Center of thePhilippines-the building developed to the arts; and MOA, the Mall of Asia, one of the largest shopping malls in Asia. They all stand on a vast reclaimed area developed during the Marcos dictatorship. The narrative also mentions the airport named after Senator Ninoy Aquino who was shot at its tarmac.

It is Christmas season in the narrative and mentioned that the Philippines has the longest celebration in the world lasting usually for four months. Decorations are set from the first "ber" month, September and hang untilthe first week of January.

3. *Structure and Style*

The novel is told in an omniscient point of view. The narrator tells the story in an all- knowing manner, with insertions of inner thoughts provided in italicized form.The stories of the characters are interwoven in the incident that happens in six consecutive days. The narrative was able to link a local incident to an international terrorist attack and eventually goes out of proportion as an issue of national security. Note in the following excerpts:

> *Palm as small as a star, star as small as a country. How small (p.10)*

> *Hush, I know a story you don't know. (p. 25)*

> *This is how the idea is infused in the story:*

It's a civilian matter, for God's sake but after 9/11 any American gets hurt or gets sneezed at in a foreign country and "terrorism" rears its ugly head. (p. 89)

Do you think this abduction could be a terrorist act against the United States? Lest you forget, we've had abductions before in Mindanao. (p.108)

Who knows, the Abu Sayyaf has now infiltrated Manila. (109)

The chronology of events is presented with some flashbacks to clarify some issues like the background of the American woman Cate Burns, the experience of Colonel David Lane in Iraq, Afghanistan and the cause of silence of the main character, Noland, including the trauma of her mother to soldiers in uniforms.

This is an example of how the narrative presented the earlier events in a whole short chapter:

The sun is high and the field is white. It's close to noon. A man is pacing around the hut, his wife pleading with him. Earlier he was in the field, fixing a water pipe; a paddy fish was caught in it. The landlord's foreman came, a surprise visit- he usually comes only during the harvest. He was friendly, even got down on his knees to help him rescue the fish. They had a laugh, then a smoke. Then slowly the news about the planned subdivision, because the landlord must diversify. The voice was apologetic, saying nothing will happen until after the next harvest and his family can stay for as long as he likes even after that, until the construction begins, of course.

The rescued fish stopped struggling in his grip. His fingers burrowed into the gills; a bone struck into his palm. The sun disappeared in the sky; even as it burned his face.

"No, you're not going there, not like this', says his wife, but even his ears have died. Only his skin feels real, stinging in every pore as he walks out, walks to the big house, just as the landlord is getting into his Mercedes for a lunch in town without his usual bodyguards.

His ears have died like his eyes, all silent and dark, but his arms, his chest, all his flesh feels the warm spurts as he hacks and hacks. This is for my son, my father, my father's father- all of us that you've erased from this land. (pp. 245- 246)

The above citation from the novel explains the earlier actions that led to the rationalization of events causing the mother and son's fate six years since then. The same is true with the socio-political issues that are mentioned in the story.

Lacan as discussed by Homer (2005) tends to associate the Imaginary with the restricted spheres of consciousness and self-awareness. It is the register with the closest links to what people experience as non- psychoanalytic quotidian reality. Who and what one "imagines" other persons to be, what one thereby "imagines" they mean when communicatively interacting, who and what one "imagines" oneself to be, including from the imagined perspectives of others—all of the preceding is encompassed under the heading of this register.

4. Tone

The way the story was told has traces of concern to the innocent victims of circumstances. The story presents the main character as helpless. Despite his struggle against their poverty, his interest on stars and angel eventually leads him to a situation worsened by people, rich and poor, in his society. The hero turns out as evil and the evil evades the crime through the power of politics.

A call for awareness on the societal issues that oppressed the already oppressed is the novel's purpose. It points to the opposite of the real problem, where non-serious matters are treated as the more serious. The tone can be clearly identified as satirical as the events pose various issues in the society from simple to complex manipulation of power. Hints of call for salvation is obvious in the presentation of how the fictional characters think for themselves, the real stories around them and the society as a whole. Below is an example of how call for salvation is presented in the narrative:

> *When a story is told, there's nothing much to do. The air does it for us, replenishes our lungs because we've lost so much in the telling, but even this air is thick with story. It feeds us back what we've just told, so it's difficult to breathe. (p. 253)*

5. Theme

The whole novel is packed with different metaphors that call attention to listening, to paying attention with the things that matter despite the idea of silence amidst war. Both mother and son longed to be heard, to have someone who will ask them and listen to their cries, to break their silence and hear what they are about to say. Moreover, the need to give focus on the issues that can only be treated with one's helpfulness is also one of the main ideas in the novel.

This is how the narrative presents such instance:

> *What happened, Nena?*

She keeps feeding the boy soup. It runs downhis chest.

Did anyone hurt you, Noland?

She is crying, It's good to be asked, ay it's good

to be asked. (p.228)

It is also the consideration of respect of individual's rights and freedom that the novel likewise wants to imply. Every character, including the mother and the son, has the desire of being free. The freedom to decideand do what they want. In the case of Noland, he only wants to sell his lantern and help the American woman whom he thinks is an angel from the sky. Nena only wants to protect her son and survive. Elvis and Bobby Cool want freedom and survival from poverty, hence the pedophile thing. Cate Burns wants to claim her freedom of keeping the baby and later, to reciprocate the goodness of those who help her. Before the murder of Germinio De Vera, he wants to expose the graft and corruption of the senator. The same concept is being pursued by the young journalist, Eugene Costa.

The other characters all desire freedom from poverty and claims for peace, (against the idea of relocation) in theirplace, the intersection. The Senator wants to free himself from the accusations of the media. ColonelDavid Lane as well as Roberto Espinosa wants their ownliberty to help, to provide justice. The former wants pursue the request of Cate Burns and personally help theinnocent victims by himself; while the latter wants to reveal the truth behind the "evidence", the notebook with mere sketches of stars.

Furthermore, the concept of Christmas offers hope and salvation through the celebrated birth of infant Jesus, whom the Catholics believed as their savior. The season proposes most positive expectations of goodwill, love, reunion, forgiveness, acceptance and generosity. Such optimistic ideas are all suggestive in the novel.

The above discussion points back to the conclusion of Lacan (2004a) that underneath the signifier is a repressed unconscious reality capable of being unveiled. He borrowed the concepts of metaphor and metonymy from Roman Jacobson in re – appropriating Freud;s condensation and displacement of ideas.

6. *Star: Its Contextual Representation*

Star is ever present in the entire novel. Star in general, represents hope and optimism. Its brightness serves as the light that illuminates the concept of darkness. Thereare various ways on how the star is used in the novel torepresent ideas.

Star for money. Parol or the Christmas Lantern is the ware that the main character sells. Star that way, servesas the main source of income that puts food on their table. It is also used by Elvis as a props whenever he needs to deliver his service to a foreign client from the pimp, Bobby Cool. The same was used by Bobby Cool to win his trust and company as a possible another protège in the future. Note this in the following excerpts:

> *Parol is the traditional star lantern. Not for Noland, Though. You call a star a star, or notat all. But of course, he can"t say. Nor can hesay that Bobby's donation of five hundred pesos towards his business is too generous.*

> *What if he can't sell enough lanterns to pay him back? But uncle and nephew assured himthat business would grow if they worked together like family. (p. 6)*

Star for Friendship. Star with five points is compared with the littleness of the palm. The little hands of Nolandand Elvis which sealed their friendship through their "gimme five" gesture. The size of the star is also compared to the smallness of the Philippines as a country and its friendly relations with the vast land of United States of America. The US flag is composed of fifty-two stars that represent the number of states. Such ideas can be deciphered from the following lines in the novel:

Palm as small as a star, star as small as a country. (p.4) They grew softer when his benefactors realized he couldn't speak. "You don't say because you're busy thinking", Elvis diagnosed his condition. "So gimme five!" Their friendship was sealed. (p.6)

Star for Hope. Star suggests hope and inspiration for Noland. He decorates their house with pictures of angels and stars from magazines and billboards. His star lanterns also inspire him and encourage him to do creative things despite being forlorn for four years. This is how it is described in the narrative:

One Christmas, he bought some Japanese paper and bamboo from money earned selling his scavenged bottles. He made his first lantern, a tiny star. By a stroke of luck, he sold it to someone who had just bought a shell lantern. He happened to be standing with his star beside one of the stalls. The nice lady thought his creation "cute" and rare these days when lanterns were made of either plastic or shell, "Parolito – little lantern", she said pinching his cheek. He couldn't name his price, but she gave him fifteen pesos. He was stunned. His mother wept and thanked his angels, not for the money but for the return of her boy. He was coming alive. He stopped whimpering into space, stopped wetting his pants. He made more stars. In this joy, all sorrow could only be irrelevant. (p. 20)

Star for Entertainment. Star City refers to the entertainment center with different rides. When Noland first saw it, his impression is it is a city inhabited by stars. Elvis tries to tell Noland that it is where they can find Ferris wheels, bumper cars, roller coasters, Little Mermaid, Snow White, Horror House. It is a place where their cart is not allowed but other types of transportation abound. The following is an excerpt of the argument between the guard and Elvis at the door of the Star city:

> *At the door, the guard stops them. He notes the shabby cart, thinks street kids. "Hoy, not allowed". "I'll pay for it, too- how much do you want?" He takes out a wad of pesos from his pocket. But the guard can't be seen to go back on hs word. "You don't pay to me, you pay there." He motions to the counter inside. But they won't let you in, so go away. You're holding up the line (p.104).*

Star for Guide. In the story referring to the Holy Family, a star guided the kings to trace the newbown Jesus. This star is represented in the nativity of the Holy Family. In the novel, the star also serves as the guide of Noland towards coming to life after realizing that he could earn money out of selling the star lanterns. The sketches of star in his notebook also provide illumination of truth to Chief Espinosa, yet others interpreted them as a cult sign.

Star for Conspiracy. The notebook of Noland with sketches of stars where each of the five points was encircled is interpreted as a cult sign. There are also speculations from their own neighbors that the mother and son are part of a cult, called kultong terorista or a terrorist cult. Initially, this is how they have interpreted the drawing which resulted to the exoneration of the real criminal. The excerpt from the narrative discusses such assumptions although ironically, an American official sees clearly the truth. Consider the following excerpts from the narrative:

In the way the star is drawn and decked, it looks like a –
what do you call it, a mandala? Is this evidence of a cult?
Was the American abducted by a cult? And the journalist
shot by their hitman? Are the boys working for a terrorist
cult? (p. 179)

"A kid, a lantern seller, is an Abu Sayyaf operative in the
slums of Manila, is that it?' "What do you think?"

He laughs bitterly. "A Hollywood conspiracy. C'mon, the
boy's hut is filled with stars and angels. He's acatholic.
It's not Allah, Bettina, it's a different God. But the spin
doctors left that out, of course. (pp 213-214)

Star for a Private Room. A five-star hotel is where the "business"
of Elvis concludes. It is also where Noland had his first exposure to
prostitution, where he was exploited by a pedophile Japanese. The
hotel room serves as Noland's witness of Elvis' supposition that
Bobby is a liar. It could be for more than pictures that the Japanese
has paid for. In another perspective, the room in a five-star hotel
indicates the only place where Elvis and Noland can get resources
for salvation.

Star for Angels. Nena told a story to the six-year old Noland that
the stars above the hill are angels and they are watching over them.
Over the years, whenever Noland collects stars, it is always
accompanied by angels. This is how the narrative describes
Noland's thoughts when his father was killed:

He's afraid there's no angel waiting up there because
there's no star yet, of course. The stickfigure is halfway up.
Sometimes it disappears, swallowed by the brightness. He
squints to bring it back. (p. 248)

Stars are used to indicate both negative and positive sides of the
picture. The things that they represent show the connotative picture

of the country, Philippines with longing for things which are foreign and looked up to. Stars suggest both hope and despair to the actual issuesof the nation that need change for the better.

It can be gleaned from the abovementioned discussion of various representation of star, that the language of literature, like the images in Freud's dreams is constantly being disguised as metaphor and metonymy.The readers' task is to unveil the literary work's latent, unconscious text from the manifest one. (Stoltfuz 1996,p.7)

7. *Societal Problems Depicted in the Novel*

Poverty is manifested in the narrative through the mention of the houses in the slums. The attitude of the neighbors towards one another is somehow suggesting an intention, or a way of liberating themselves from poverty. Every character who lives in the intersection is wary of one another. For instance, Helen suspects that Manang Betya pocketed her winning once; and Liza hasalso hijacked her laundry customer.

The issue of gambling is also evident even in the intersection at the midst of crisis amidst the Christmas season and fear of the "relocation". There is the mentionthat Mario won in the cockfight, thus Helen was able tocook chicken tinola out of his winning. The mention of jueteng is an explicit example of gambling where people bet money for a game of luck in their chosen numbers.

Child prostitution is clearly manifested in the narrative.Bobby Cool has been a child prostitute before he founda protégé through Elvis. Elvis succumbs to the "business" to survive and to enjoy simple pleasures likegoing to the mall, wearing fake branded apparels, and treating Noland with some of his "profit". Bobby deceptively introduced Noland in the same business andit angers Elvis.

The problems met by OFW's like the wife of Mang Gusting and

Mikmik's mother who went to Hongkong to work as a domestic helper is also implied in the story. The domino effect of having no woman in the family can lead to extra marital affair and an unusual personality of a child.

Issues on morality are not as much practiced by the poor, but more so by those in power and even government officials. As mentioned in this descriptive statement lifted from the novel: A businessman and his mistress sit up in bed, awed by the helicopter with a machine gun hanging out right at their hotel window. (p.91)

The issue of greed extends not only to the insatiability on money but also of power. The senator uses his connections not to lose his power, gained through obtaining money from gambling and other illegal activities. The unending war can also be traced from the greed of power.

CONCLUSIONS AND RECOMMENDATIONS

The Solemn Lantern Maker is full of urban-centered scenes with some flashes of a farm life that provide obvious contrast and similarity between the two. The desperate hope of those in the city fearing of eviction from their "borrowed lands" and their way of life presents a resemblance with that of those in the rural, in the farm, cultivating one's land for their living. The novel calls for hope despite the traumatic experiences from the societal cancer, the hegemony of power

The name Noland portrays the literal situation, "no land". An incident in the past related to land when he was just six years old causes his trauma that results to his "silence". The land in the narrative symbolizes not only a farm or a residential lot but a larger perspective of a country.

Holland (1968) in his The Dynamics of Literary Response considers that the literary text is decoded to reveal how disguise and adaptation into socially acceptable language serve to make unconscious wishes accessible to the reader through creative transformation. This is manifested in the novels of Bobis where she presents ideas about her own country compared with her experiences in other country.

The theme of freedom and identity in the novel can also be hinted from the idea of love. This idea of love was also evident in the other novels of Bobis as mentioned by Gilbas (2015) in her discussion of satirical tropes. From the novel's analysis, this is clearly evident in the major character's trauma that resulted to his "silence" which can be traced back from his father's love. The arrival of the American, Cate Burns who was called the "angel" was triggered by her love to her unborn child. The love for "peace" of the other characters manipulated their actions and connivance to the extent of sabotage and salvage.

The idea of phenomenology as discussed by Hornedo (2002) states that "there is a human nature common to writer and reader. Thus the phenomenological intentional acts described by a writer in his work, even if fictive, since these have been present to another's consciousness, they can become present again in another's". It was further explained that the said idea makes it possible for the reader to "re- experience the work in his or her own consciousness".

The Solemn Lantern Maker, star and angel are the tropes which also become the source of problem in the narrative. They signify the opposite of the novel's theme. They are hope and guidance that the characters' need most. Those tropes also represent various incidental socio-cultural and political involvement of the country. Also, the tropes let the readers decipher and trace the historical journey of the Philippines from the colonizers. Both the star and angel of Noland can be accounted to the Catholic religion that gives hints of Spanish influence and at the same time American supremacy over a developing country like the Philippines.

The narrative is a showcase of the nation's societal exploration where people's dreams are silenced by their experiences, psychological intricacies and external power or forces. It is suggested that fictive stories be treated with analyses that may elevate the literary work from a simply "reading for pleasure material" to a culturally specific context that abounds with historical and universal truths exposing human conditions.

REFERENCES

Bobis M. (2008) The solemn lantern maker, Manila: Anvil Publishing Inc.

Grosz E. (2001) Jacques Lacan: A feminist introduction. New York: Rouledge.

Gilbas, S. A. (2015). Satire in the Novels of Merlinda Bobis (Doctoral dissertation, University of Santo Tomas).

Holland, N. (1968) The dynamics of literary response. USA. University of Florida

Homer, S. (2005) Jacues Lacan. the Rouledge Critical Thinkers, London and New York: Taylor and Francis Grp.

Hornedo F. (2003) The phenomenology of freedom. Manila. UST Publishing House

Lacan J. (2004) "The Mirror Stage as Formative ofthe I Function, as Revealed in Psychoanalytic Experience" Ecrits: A Selection. Bruce Fink, trans. New York: Norton

Lacan J. (2004) The Subversion of the Subject andthe Dialectic of Desire in the Freudian Unconcious.Ecrits: A Selection: Bruce Fink, trans. New York: Norton

Stolzfuz B. (1996) Lacan and Literature: Purloined Pretexts. New York: State University of New York Press.

Tomsic,S. and Zevnik A. eds. (2016)Jacques Lacan: Between Psychoanalysis and Politics. New York: Rouledge.

5

The Devices of Satire in Bobis' *Fish Hair Woman*: A Call for Change

Published in Asia Pacific Social Science 19(1) 2018
ISSN 01198386

According to Lumbera (1997, p. 58), readinga literary work requires one to "engage with its language as the social practice of individuals, groups and institutions." He referred to Philippine literature as that which "may be produced in the capital city of Manila and in the different urban centers and rural outposts, even in foreign lands where descendants ofFilipino migrants use English or any of the languagesof the Philippines to create works that tell about theirlives and aspirations"(p.59). This goes to show that the novels though written in another country and ina foreign language may still serve as good sources of material on Philippine studies. Furthermore, Lumbera(1997) said:

> The forms used by Filipino authors may be indigenous or borrowed from other cultures, and these may range from popular pieces addressed to mass audiences to highly sophisticated worksintended for the intellectual elite. (p. 2)

This paper highlights the work of Merlinda Bobis.She is a poet before she became a fictionist. She is atransnational artist whose works primarily concerns Philippine culture. Bobis' prose, such as short storiesand novels, was published when she was already working in Australia as a Creative Writing professor.She left for Australia in 1991, under a scholarshipto pursue her doctorate degree after her 11 years ofteaching in different institutions in the Philippines. Onthe third year of her doctorate program in Australia, she applied for a teaching job, got it, and at the time of thiswriting, she is still working at Wollongong University.I focused on Bobis' (2012) *Fish-Hair Woman,* that may somewhat fall under an epistolary novel.The epistolary technique is evident in the first partof the novel which is called the longest love-letter toher "beloved." The novel has five parts and the othertwo later parts are told by an unknown narrator, froman omniscient point of view. Just like the other twoearlier novels, it can be identified as a social novel. It emphasizes the influence of the social and economicconditions of an era in shaping characters anddetermining events. Often, it also embodies implicit orexplicit problems recommending political and social reforms.

Satire, as Abrams (1999, p. 275) defined it, "is the literary art of diminishing or derogating a subject by making it ridiculous and evoking toward it attitudes of amusement, contempt, scorn, or indignation." It isdifferentiated from the comic which comedy evokes as laughter serving mainly as an end in itself while satire ridicules and uses laughter as a weapon, and against a butt that exists outside the work itself. The aesthetics of satire can be identified through the theme and tone. Abrams (1999) further explained this view in the following statements:

Satire occurs as an incidental element within many works whose overall mode is not satiric in a certain character or situation, or in an interpolated passage of ironic commentary on some aspect of the human condition or of contemporary society. The most common indirectform is that of a fictional narrative, in which theobjects of the satire are characters who make themselves and their opinions ridiculous orobnoxious by what they think, say, and do, andare sometimes made even more ridiculous by theauthor's comments and narrative style. (p.277)

It is evident that Bobis experimented on forms and applies whatever she thinks is useful in her craft as acreative writer and professor. In whatever form, shehas maintained a certain desire to criticize society.Her works consistently focus on the call for hope and change against the social, political, and cultural issues. This study's objective is to identify the type of satire, style, and devices in Bobis' third novel. It alsoaims to reveal how Bobis literarily criticizes societythrough the aesthetics of satire and her adept use oftropes as the representation of ideas. I intended to provethat Bobis' novel presents criticisms of the societywhere her consciousness on the region, in particular, and the country, in general, is anchored. My pointof contention is that Bobis writes literarily in a waythat the readers see the flaws of the society, yet offerssolution or possibility of cure and hope to the exposed social problems.

METHODS

This paper utilizes a formalistic approach in the analyses of *Fish-Hair Woman,* the third novel ofMerlinda Bobis (2012). It won for her three awards such as the Most Underrated Book award in 2013, finalist for *Davitt Awards* under the *Best Crime and Mystery Books by Australian Women* during the sameyear; and winner of *Juan C. Laya Prize* as Best Novel in a foreign language in 2014. The applied approach covers the descriptive-qualitative type of literary criticism.

Theoretical Background

This study employed Hornedo's (2002, p. 42) ideathat "to an extent, the artist is an artifact of culture, andwhat art discloses is not an individual consciousness but a narrative larger than the individual's personal narrative of himself." Hornedo's statement asserts that a piece of literature reflects the worldview of its writer, which is the result of personal experiences, basically rooted from culture. I, therefore, anchored this study's argument on the idea that Bobis is a satirist, a Filipino expatriate writer who also considers herself as a transnational of Australia. Her novels are reflective of how she views Philippine society in general and the Bicolanos in particular. Through the aesthetics and devices of satire, this research sought to disclose that Bobis writes about her society for its people to recognize the need to change and become aware of the problems that arise from individual and societal behavior. Through her works, Bobis induces calls for change that may emanate from the people who may see themselves being implicitly represented by the characters in the novels.

Overview

The novel starts with the "longest love letter" of Estrella titled "Beloved." She claims herself as the fish-hair woman who uses her 12-meter-long hair to retrieve corpses from her village—Iraya's river. The manuscript reveals her personal life leading up to the war and the war itself. Estrella is the illegitimate daughter of the former mayor Estradero (Doctor Alvarado). Her mother, Carmen, was only 15 years old and died during childbirth. Mamay Dulce, the attending midwife, adopts her after the death of her grandmother soon after her mother's. Being naturally bald at birth, Pay Inyo the gravedigger, *herbolario,* and perpetual suitor of Mamay Elena, helps grow Estrella's hair through his incantations and herbal medicines. The hair "miraculously" grows along with painful memories, after Estrella's near-death experience at the age of five.

Pilar and Bolodoy, Mamay Dulce's children, face life's turn when each chooses the "left", joins the communist insurgent, and "right" the private army. It breaks their mother's heart and literally kills her.

Those incidents happen when Estrella and Adora, the orphan and niece of the *Jueteng* queen, are in Hawaii with ex-governor Estradero.

The rest of the novel, Parts Four and Five, are told by an unnamed narrator and examines how the events of the manuscript are dealt with in the present by Estrella (now as Stella), Luke, and a litany of other characters. By this time Pilar and Tony, the Australian journalist whom both Pilar and Estrella had loved, are among the dead or disappeared. The novel was centered on *Tony's* mysterious disappearance in the Philippines.

Tony's 19-year-old son, Luke, was lured to the Philippines on the pretext that his father is alive, by Kiko who wishes to "sanitize" history and facilitate his return to politics. There he met Adora, the mute lady, and fell in love with her silence. Dr. Alvarado's death puts the village at peace and the other characters at rest.

There are too familiar stories in the novel. They are stories of farmers' expropriation, being pushed off their land and turned into landless wage laborers by power-greedy *mestizo* elites like Dr. Alvarado, alias Governor Estradero and his private army, the *Anghel de la Guardia.* There are also stories of rape, torture, and murder by the State with the complicit backing of the West, including Australia.

The story transcends through three decades and continents. It covers events from 1977 to 1997, from Philippine village Iraya to Australia and Hawaii. The novel ends with an epilogue of father and daughter's vacation in Iraya, where Luke and Addie, Adora's daughter, were enveloped in the light of fireflies.

The analyses are divided into two parts, (1) the discussion of the techniques and devices of satire and (2) the presentation of tropes used in the novel. The second part is deemed important to identify the figurative representation of the ideas that the author would like to impart to her readers. The tropes are likewise used in revealing the satirical designs appliedin the narrative.

RESULTS

The Techniques and Devices of Satire in the Novel

Exaggeration. The length of Estrella's hair, 12 meters long, is an exaggerated representation of the span of her memory and how long it grows with one handspan. Moreover, the connection of the hair to theheart is an example of the exaggeration technique in the novel that satirizes history through hair as memory andthe heart as longing for love. The following excerpts express the said ideas:

> Everytime I remembered anything that unsettledmy heart, my hair grew one handspan. MamayDulce was convinced of this phenomenon whenI was six years old. 'very tricky hair, very trickyheart', she whispered to me in her singsong onmornings when I woke up to even longer hair on my pillow after a night of agitated dreams. (Bobis, 2012, p. 3)

> You see, Mamay Dulce, history hurts my hair, did you know that? Remembering is always a bleeding out of memory, like pulling thread from a vein in the heart, a coagulation so fine, miles of it stretching upwards to the scalp then sprouting there into the longest strand of red hair. Some face-saving tale to explain my twelve meters of very thick black hair with its streaks of red and hide my history. (Bobis, 2012, p. 4)

> How much can the heart accommodate? Death and love, an enemy and a sweetheart, war and an impassioned serenade, and more. Only four chambers, but with infinite space like memory where there is room even for those whom we do

not love. (Bobis, 2012, p. 142)

The philosophical representation of the capillaries of the heart, love and hatred are connected to the veins of the scalp where the hair meets with memory that tells history. Estrella reveals the history through her memories and nostalgic stories that aim to provide justice to the oppressed. Ten years after the Total War in the Philippines, stories written in Hawaii were sent to the Philippines through an Australian character. He
was asked to open the case of a lost Australian reporter, who is apparently the letter sender's lover.

Incongruity. The use of "my house" referring to the place where one of the political characters, Mayor Reyes, stays shows a paradoxical idea. He offers his house as open to the people, claiming himself as the people's mayor who came from the hills and served their cause. "My house is open to you" (Bobis, 2012, p.263). This house is actually the Alvarados/Estraderos' which was vacated when the former governor fled to Hawaii. Being the biggest house in Iraya that boasted power, the newly elected mayor, once a revolutionary, requested "to rent" the ancestral house. The following lines may strengthen the abovementioned ideas:

> Mayor Reyes is not quite a tenant. He arranged the transfer of domicile with Iraya's local government six years ago. After he was sworn on his first term, he argued that the mayor must be stationed in the most presentable house in the village, for the time being, of course. Until he has arranged for a residence that is worthy of the position: something with a decent representation to the public. (Bobis, 2012, p. 259)

In the Philippines, particularly in rural areas, political figures are always expected to have a better kind of living than their constituents. In the case of the current mayor, he uses his position to meet his personal needs and at the same time enjoy the "power" given by the mass of people.

The character of Rizalino "Bolodoy" Capaz, labeled as "Bolodoy the terrible" clearly manifests anexample of incongruity in his mental ability as well as physical aspect. The name *Bolodoy* either suggestsa hill-hillbilly or a dumb-dumbbell. His real name, Rizalino, was patterned after the Filipinos' national hero known as intelligent in all aspect. In one of Bolodoy's third-grade classroom experiences at 12 years old, he associated letter B for *buyod,* a local term for shrimp. When he was told by the teacher to "go and plant kamote'" he proudly responded that hewas already doing it and he produces the best *duma,* orsweet potatoes in their farm. Below is the excerpt ofthe narrative that describes the said classroom scenario:

> An uncouth, ignorant, atrocious hick, de primera clase, one of his teachers confided to a colleagueduring his third grade, after he came to class with a bag of shrimps. The story goes that he sweated over the alphabets beside that poor teacher who, while agonizing over his total inability to recognize the strange markings on paper, also suffered a jumping thing inside herblouse. Which he quickly retrieved with his handin a flash. B is for buyod- shrimp! Between histeacher's bosom!
>
> Sorry ma'am, sorry, they're very fresh that's why, just caught them in the river this morning, ay so very sorry ma'am.
>
> Thus he was expelled during his third grade; hewas twelve.
>
> You better go home and plant kamote, theteacher screamed.
>
> I'm already planting them ma'am. But in my family, we call them duma, more proper that way. (Bobis, 2012, p. 184)

It was further mentioned in the narrative that the worst insult anyone can receive at school is "you better go home and plant sweet potatoes." It meant that one's intellect was as lowly as the humble tuber,which does not need any particular mental acumento grow.

Agriculture is considered as a low type of occupation in the country; thus, the insult goes with the idea that planting is the only possible occupation in his lifetime and the person is not meant to do other complex human concerns.

Another instance that shows incongruity is when Pilar uses teasing ditty as one way of getting the attention of her Mamay Dulce. Pay Inyo serenades his love with the help of the three children to no avail. This is the teasing ditty that Pilar sings at the top of her lungs:

> Mapula-pula pisngi ni Dulsora
> Very red the cheeks of Dulsora
> Tugtog mambo-jambo the music is mambo-jambo
>
> Kabit ni Pay Inyo
> She's dancing with Pay Inyo (Bobis, 2012,p. 141)

In the Philippines, it is unusual that children teasethe adult in an uncourteous way. In that instance, it was effective because Mamay Dulce appeared at the window to find and punish Pilar, an action which confirmed that the latter's intention was served. The "serenaders" saw her apparition at the window. It is a common fact that the children's favor is first soughtin wooing the adult, such as the case of Mamay Dulceand Pay Inyo. The narrator recounts the process in thefollowing lines:

> The serenade went on for too long and too desperately. We nearly outgrew the old man's stratagems in the art of village courtship. Turutalinga, dilimon, labyu, tira-tira, balicucha and all delights available in his glass jars werethe palate-sweeteners for us children. Flowered housedress, tortoise-shell comb, rosy lipstick orsequined velvet sandals from the city were theheart-implorers for dear Mamay Dulce. These were the gifts that he brought on his regular courting hour, three to four on a Saturday afternoon. He never visited without presents. (Bobis, 2012, p. 141)

Despite the long and extended courtship, it was not reciprocated. Ironically, because of love, Mamay Dulce cannot accept the offered love of her only suitor. She considers it sacrificial not to marry and as she explains to Pay Inyo, "because of the kids;I'm afraid the heart has very little room" (Bobis, 2012, p.142).

Parody. Estrella is literally born bald, which troubles people around her. They provide collective efforts to help grow her hair. There are several suggestions, mostly to pray novenas to particularpatron saint along with the concoctions of herbs in her head. One of the raised options is to offer five novenas to Santa Maria Magdalena. Another option is to praya novena to Saint Jude, the saint of lost causes, and the other is to pray to Saint Rita, the patron saint for impossible wishes.

All the said ideas were opposed with different reasons. It was considered that while Santa Magdalenais in the Holy Book, she is also the whore, referred to as "the fallen woman with beautiful hair"(p. 61). "She became a saint when she washed His feet with perfumeand her hair" (p. 62). It angered Mamay Dulce the ideathat the hairlessness of Estrella is a lost cause and animpossible case.

It was emphasized in the above discussion that people offer novena prayers for specific intentions, but faith may only help if there is acceptance along with it. For every patron saint suggested, there is always the opposing idea that argues with the intention. It is abitter fact that the believers have their own argumentsbetween logic and faith. It can also be noted that ruralfolks in their desperation, have nothing else to rely onbut the medicines from nature and what was left of their faith.

An example of travesty evident in the narrativeis the idea of "angelhood." It was described that"angelhood is every little girl's dream in Iraya" (p. 69). The angel's task is to unveil the mourning

Blessed mother with hands folded in prayer whileshe is being lowered in mid-air, a rope tied on her waist and sings *Salve Regina.* In Iraya, "angelhood isexpensive" because the search for the angel is done through money-contest. The details are presented in the following excerpt from the narrative:

> The race towards angelhood was expensive and ate up precious time. It meant winning a money-contest or, kindly put, assisting the church in its fund-raising project. In this worthy task,the stage mothers of the six-to eight years old aspirants compete in selling the most number of tickets, in the name of their daughters. The biggest earner wins the title of "angel." (Bobis,2012, p. 70)

The grandiose idea of being an angel is sought, but the significance is sacrificed and neglected inthe process. Popularity and finances count the most rather than the essence of the angel's representation. The adults promote their children, which results to boost of pride or disappointment, either way of their own children or the others. The supposedly religious
activity expected to promote values encourages the opposite. Being an angel does not require excellence in attitude or character, as long as their parents have enough money. The church initiates if not tolerates thesaid practice.

Reversal. The use of a white man, Australian writerTony, to dig up and search for history instead of a nativeFilipino, such as the self-acclaimed fish- hair woman's very own sister, Pilar, is a manifestation of reversal. The first-person narrator, the letter sender writes storiesabout her village and persuades Luke, the son of Tony, to visit the Philippines. The ulterior motive is not forLuke to search for his father but to seek justice for those who have been victims of militarization and insurgency. If the stories in the series of letter intend to trace the history of the Philippines using a native Filipino who has been lost, nobody may lift a finger, but if it concerns a white man, it calls attention; thus,the strategy of Estrella. Notice the following lines in the narrative, a conversation scene between another Australian, Mr. Baker, and a Filipino professor, Inez Carillo:

> But Estrella Capili's story is bigger than the white man, the white man is no hero here, the white man is only a prop to tell her story. And he's stereotyped, even ridiculed, so shouldn't I then complain as a white man? I mean- this is not his story! For once, he reverses the lecturing tone. This, Professor, is the story of a whole village, about someone's memory. (Bobis, 2012,p. 228)

The professor also claimed that Estrella turned her back from the village, from her family, and her country.Prof Carillo believes that her high school classmate andbest friend left her and her own heart, off to another country with her biological father who is considered asthe most corrupt governor of the country. She considers that the stories are intended for Estrella's vindication and not to serve justice to the victims. It is very evidentthat Prof. Carillo is not convinced of Mr. Baker's assertion on the fish-hair woman's letter. Instead, shelet logic be carried away by emotions. These are herwords to Mr. Baker:

> Remember this: she wasn't even here during ourTotal war. She left us all in the seventies, thenwrote herself clean in this manuscript. She haswritten herself in the place of her sister, and inthe place of a myth- you know, Mr. Baker, in 1987 Iraya did believe in a Fish-Hair Woman.Despair makes you believe in anything. It fuelsfervor, it is its own religion. (Bobis, 2012, pp. 228–229)

Reversal as an idea can be figured out from the styleof the author in presenting the details in the narrative. A Filipino highlight a foreigner, a foreigner who rather believes a Filipino, and a Filipino who despisesanother Filipino.

The definition of the word salvage as presentedin the narrative is another example of reversal. Accordingly, its original meaning comes from the Latin word, *salvare,* referring to rescue, retrieve, or preserve from loss or destruction. It was mentioned thatin the narrator's village, the word is "whispered witha weigh in the tongue, sinking the word like a body thrown into the river" (p. 38). The new definition of the word salvage is the opposite of its actual meaning.In Iraya, it refers to liquidated, made liquid, or made to disappear and summarily executed.

Defamiliarization. The use of magico-tale ofa woman with 12-meter long hair is, by itself, a defamiliarization. The use of magic-realism is evidentin the narrative. Notice in the following excerpts:

We went, a grim recession to the river, guarded by flying lights and the soldiers who held my hair like a bridal train. Again, I remembered his lips and the precious stones on my back and the river in my pelvis and his lemon grass fish swimming from the belly of a dead girl now growing her face and nipples back and her grandmother rubbing her feet as if tryingto remember something and the soft mound of earth singing the ten-year old bones to sleep. (Bobis, 2012, p.16)

A strung of hair is flung out the window. It gets caught in the wind. (Bobis, 2012, p. 52)

He is at sea with Adora. He has just shampooedhis hair when they set afloat in what looks likehalf a boat. No, it is a couch with a sail. They reach the middle of the sea where the water is clear and still. He wants to wash off the shampoofrom his hair, but there's only salt water and itwon't do.

He asks, 'Does my father know about me?'

Adora does not answer. She jumps off the boatand disappears. He is suddenly alone, holding alittle bucket. The sea is so clear, it will suffice.He dips into it with his bucket and pours the water on his head to wash off the shampoo. Hishead begins to itch. He scratches it, but itches even more. The itch is growing bigger, the itchinfects his fingers. He looks at them- there are maggots under his nails! His hair is full of maggots! He must wash them off, so he dips for more water, but it's no longer clear. It has dimmed with maggots. He panics. He must washhis hair, he must!

But each time he dips into the water, the maggotsmultiply. He begins to howl. Then he feels a fainttickle in his ear.

It is a maggot whispering, "Does your father know about me? (Bobis, 2012, pp. 99–100)

The first excerpt refers to the collective memory of Estrella about the military, both the government and the revolutionary side. They both abuse their power to the wanton loss of civilian lives. It emphasizes thatthe victims are still very young but have been deprivedof a good future.

On the other hand, the maggots represent the secretsor hidden ideas from Luke which he starts to uncoverand realize. They are the truth behind the letters and the stories he receives. They are just in front of him and even if he tries to avoid, he has already committedhimself to know and expose them.

Tropes in the Novel-Hair and its ContextualRepresentation

The novel talks about memory as presented throughhair and river that refer to glamour and source of lifeor living. It is ironic that the river, which supposedlyrepresents life, is the place where the dead bodiescan be found. They are fished-out by the hair which symbolizes memory. The hair also called the "crowningglory" of every woman is deliberately used to trawl the corpses from the river. The tropes are used to recount the different periods in the Philippines and the influences of other countries. The dark and the bright sides of the Philippine experiences, as well as the negative and positive culture of people, are highlightedthrough the representation of hair as memory and theriver as a continuous battle for liberation from the past.

Hair for Memory

Estrella's hair is a metaphorical allusion to memory.Her entire history is represented through the length ofher hair. The "longest hair" is a combination of socialand magic realism. She helps find and give justice to theoppressed from far Hawaii to the river of Iraya throughthe stories created out of her memory. At the beginning of the novel, the first-person narrator describes Estrella and her hair in the following lines:

> Hair. How was it linked with the heart? I'll tellyou- it had something to do with memory. Every time I remembered anything that unsettled my heart, my hair grew one handspan. MamayDulce was convinced of this phenomenon whenI was six years old. "Very tricky hair. very trickyheart', she whispered to me in her singsong onmornings when I woke up to even longer hair on my pillow after a night of agitated dreams. (Bobis, 2012, p. 5)

Estrella was born bald which signifies that, at birth, she is free from any story or memory. "It is 1959, summertime and I am born bald" (Bobis, 2012, p. 29).As she grows older, her hair grows along with stories.In her letter to Tony, it says, "I want to wrap you in my hair, these strands that would not stop growing into story after story, into all that I remember of my village in 1987 and the years before. Stories that can save, thatcan kill" (Bobis, 2012, p. 137). Her scalp aches with the torture of stories which identify her roots.

Hair for Cure

Just as hair represents memory, it also symbolizesremedy or cure. Estrella is labeled as The Fish-Hair Woman, who trawls corpses from the river Irayathrough her 12-metre hair. The narrative describes her in the following verses:

Lambat na itom na itom	very black net pero sa dugo
natumtom	but blood soakedsamong babying
parasira	our fisherwomanbuhok
pangsalbar- pangsira	hair to save-fish kang samong
mga padaba	all our beloved
	(Bobis, 2012, p. 5)

"I trawled not the Australian but history" (Bobis, 2012, p. 201). This statement of Stella as the first person narrator directly reveals how she uses the hairas a representation of memory to provide a cure or help the victims of power abuse attain justice. The following lines strengthened the said idea:

It was the Total War. The military's operation Lambat Bitag: Fishnet Trap. Our village was trapped between the military's purge of the insurgency and the insurgents' purge of their own ranks, which extended to the cities and throughout the country. Between the right and the left ventricle of this constricted heart of a nation, the village conjured another net. Ten years after my brother died, I became their Fish- Hair Woman. (Bobis, 2012, p. 200)

CONCLUSIONS

In the novel under study, love is the probable cause of every event and action of the characters. Thenarrator's love for her village obliges her to claim herself as the "fish-hair woman." Her intention is to liberalize the victims of oppression and provide justicethrough stories written from her memory.

This narrative of Bobis (2012) serves as communicators of Philippine culture and history that emanate from the type of love that a Filipino has to offer and yet to have. She uses the characters and events, although fictive, in revealing the ugly points of Filipinos. According to Hornedo (2000a) in his overview of Anthropology, "every cultural community, large or small, understands itself in the frame of its own narrative or account of itself. All cultures are assumed to have their own narratives of themselves. To understand them is to understand their narrative" (p. 20).

Moreover, based from Hornedo's (2000a) discussion of the theory and the genesis of a literary text, it was explained that "the creation of a literary work is guided consciously or unconsciously by what the author thinks literature ought to achieve, to be made of, to look like and by whom" (p.73). Hence, Bobis' (2012) novel appeal to the reading Filipinos to act on their societal problems presented in a literary way through intellectual humor, not only to laugh at their own idiocies. Likewise, she also targeted other reading nationalities for possible support.

Based on the abovementioned ideas, it can be gleaned that Bobis sees her country's need for liberation and search for cultural strength. Her being transnational motivates her to write from her perspective of Philippine culture associated with her personal experiences in another country. She wants her readers to understand the novels from the recognition of society behind the creative representation of political and cultural flaws.

This study may also be used as additional source material in the Philippine culture or related subjects offered in some academes/institutions. The tools of satire may be considered as effective methods of explaining and understanding Filipino culture.

REFERENCES

Abrams, M. H. (1999). *A glossary of literary terms* (7th ed.). Cornell. Cornell University.

Bobis, M. (2012). *Fish-hair woman.* Manila, Philippines: Anvil Publishing Inc.

Hornedo, F. H. (2000a). *Culture and community in the Philippine fiesta and other celebrations.* Manila, Philippines: UST Publishing House.

Hornedo, F. H. (2000b). *The power to be. A phenomenology of freedom.* Manila, Philippines: UST Publishing House. Hornedo, F. H. (2002). *Pagpapakatao and other essays in contemporary philosophy and literature of ideas.* Manila, Philippines: UST Publishing House.

Lumbera, B. (1997). *Revaluation 1997: Essays on Philippine literature, cinema & popular culture.* Manila, Philippines: UST Publishing House.